TODAY'S TREASURES
TOMORROW'S ANTIQUES
THE HANDMADE ARTIST DOLL: 1975-2000

By Florence Theriault

Gold Horse Publishing

To order additional copies contact:
Dollmasters
PO Box 2319
Annapolis, MD 21404
Tel. 800-966-3655, Fax 410-571-9605
www.dollmasters.com

This book is based upon a collection of dolls
auctioned by Theriault's of Annapolis, Maryland.

Design by Travis Hammond
Photography by Gerald Nelson

$49
ISBN: 1-931503-34-6
Printed in Hong Kong

INTRODUCTION

To be inspired by the past, yet to see and create with one's own eye, is how one might describe the goal of late 20th century doll artists. Keen collectors recognize this and include a selection of fine contemporary artist dolls with their artful collection of antique dolls. This blend of new and old can be a delightful and harmonious juxtaposition.

One collector who has understood for many years this connection between the new and the old, the artist doll and the antique doll, is Shirley Bertrand of Illinois. Early on, she began to gather fine antique dolls, study them, and learn to distinguish quality from the mundane, real art from mere sentimentality. Then, during her annual trips to the International Toy Fair in New York where today's artists presented their dolls, she began to see that the same principles of choice used in selecting antique dolls could be applied to artist dolls. Like all great collectors who bravely move ahead of the pack, Shirley Bertrand began to gather what she considered the finest models of the new doll artists. She chose the dolls of New York state artist, R. John Wright, as her focal collection, and over the years assembled a remarkable group of dolls that she documented in her book, *Characters of R. John Wright*, published in 2000. The collection numbers more than 100 different examples including early Vermont models with wonderful highly characterized features, Little Children Series, Childhood Classics Series, Bears, One-of-a-Kinds, and Exclusive editions for specialty doll shops or conventions.

Other artists who are represented here include Regina Sandreuter, Maggie Iacono, Sylvia Natterer, Helen Kish, Edna Daly, Paul Crees, Lynne & Michael Roche, Avigail Brahms, Brigitte Deval, Hildegard Gunzel, Kathy Redmond, Jane Davies, Wendy Lawton and others. In many cases, a retrospective of the artist's work over a period of time provides a fascinating look at evolution of style and technique. Which period of the artist's work is the most sought may change with the decades, just as collectors of Picasso waver from time to time in their preference for Blue Period or Cubism. Indeed, which of today's artist will prove to be tomorrow's star remains a delightful mystery for all lovers of that animated sculpture known as a doll. In the meantime they are ours to enjoy.

Dolls by R. John Wright: The Shirley Bertrand Collection

The American doll artist created his first dolls in 1976, made of stitch-shaped wool felt. These very rare folk art style dolls were soon followed by a series of felt dolls with faces shaped by steam-sculpting and hand-painted. This was a production method that the artist has refined to a perfect art, creating over the next quarter century dozens of exceptional studio art dolls. His artistic skills have been rivaled by his imagination; the dolls have ranged from childhood friends to fantasy creatures, from whimsical old folks to storybook heroes. An insistence on quality of workmanship and materials adds to their value.

R. John and Susan Wright, partners in the studio firm, credit earlier doll makers with inspiration, whether it be the caricature dolls of the Steiff firm of Germany that he played with as a child, or the studio dolls of 1930's era makers such as Lenci. Certainly, the use of felt material with its malleable textures is an obviously seen influence, but even more important is the insistence on only the best quality of material in all aspects of production – the best wool felt dyed in the most vibrant colors, the well-chosen accessory, the softest wig even if it be hidden under a wonderful hat, the final detail of a beautiful box and label. Antique collectors, wishing to find a contemporary doll that symbolizes the timelessness of traditional studio dolls, need look no further than the R. John Wright Dolls.

The dolls appearing as #1-128 in this book are all works by R. John Wright Dolls, from the private collection of Shirley Bertrand, author of *Characters of R. John Wright*, published in 2000.

Hans Brinker's skates.

1. Hans Brinker with Jointed Knees
20". Of molded felt with unusually well defined sculpting of facial features and detailed painting including spiral threaded eyes, glazed lower lip, pouty expression, plump cheeks, blonde mohair tousled curls, jointing at shoulders and hips, and unusual jointing at the knees. He wears taupe felt jacket with patches, print collar, shirt, knit scarf, teal blue felt knickers with patches, matching cap, brown woolen stockings, black leather ankle boots and carries a pair of wooden skates with metal blades. The doll is stamped R. John Wright on left foot and has original paper label on pants "R. John Wright/ Hans Brinker/Children's Classics/ No. 048/350", and is contained in original labeled and numbered box. Hans Brinker was produced from 1990-1992 in a numbered edition of 350 dolls, and is a matched number companion to Gretel, the following doll. $1000/1500

2. Gretel Brinker
18". Of molded felt, highly characterized plump face with appealing worried expression and fine artistic painting, light brown hair with ringlet side curls, jointing at shoulder and hips. Gretel is wearing a brown felt patched dress over white blouse, with blue felt short jacket, apron, plaid neck scarf, petticoat, pantalets, wooden shoes, white coiffe, and carries an armload of sticks for the fireplace. The doll is stamped R. John Wrist on her left foot and has original paper label on her petticoat "R. John Wright/Gretel Brinker/Children's Classics/No.048/350" and is contained in original labeled and numbered box. The doll was produced from 1990-1992 in a numbered edition of 350 dolls. $1000/1500

3. Seth, from Early Character Doll Series

17". Of molded felt with characterized features, wide beaming smile, prominent nose, brown eyes set into deep sockets, and high cheek bones, Seth is crowned with very full dark brown hair and beard with a sprinkle of grey. He is jointed at shoulders and hips and wears a plaid cotton shirt, woolen pants with suspenders, tucked inside high leather boots with lace fronts, brown felt hat, and carries a four-prong wooden pitchfork. The doll has Wright stamp on its foot, and paper labels with Vermont address, identifying the doll as "Seth" and "S1-102". The model was produced from 1978-1981 only. $1500/1800

4. Emma, from Early Character Doll Series

17". Of molded feat with elongated character face, laughter crinkles around the eyes, smiling expression, brightly painted eyes, brown thick hair with grey flecks drawn into loop at back of head, Emma has especially fine detail of sculpting. She is jointed at shoulders and hips. Emma wears a moss green felt dress with brown piping, brown calico print apron, red scarf, petticoat, pantalets, brown felt shoes, and carries a broom. The doll has Wright stamp on its foot. The model was produced from 1979 to 1981 only. $1000/1400

5. St. Nicholas from Character Doll Series

18". Of molded felt with distinctively modeled features, broad nose bridge, eye laughter crinkles, hand-painted features, jointed at shoulders and hips, St. Nicholas has very full and fluffy white mohair wig, moustache and beard. He is wearing a moss green felt tunic over woven pants, tall brown felt boots, brown felt neck scarf, maroon felt hooded coat with faux-fur edging, and carries a cross and paisley velvet gift bag. The doll has Wright stamp on its foot and paper label "R. John Wright St. Nicholas No.225", and is contained in its original labeled box. The model was produced in 1979-1981 in an edition of 250. $1000/1300

7. Rosemary from Babes in Toyland, Series I, #1 of the Edition

17". Pressed felt face with painted features, blue eyes, painted lashes at upper right eye rims only, wistful expression, brunette mohair wig with tousled bangs and short braids, jointed at shoulders and hips. She wears a long grey felt night gown with white edging and cuffs, white cotton shift, pink felt slippers and hair bows, and carries a small felt doll with calico gown and bonnet. The doll is marked on her left foot, and has two original paper labels on her gown, one labeled "R. John Wright Babes in Toyland Rosemary/No.1/50", and is contained in her original labeled box with folded card reading "Babes in Toyland, Rosemary". The model was produced in 1983 only in an edition of 50, and is a numbered partner with Timothy, the following doll. $1500/2200

8. Timothy from Babes in Toyland, Series I, #1 of the Edition

17". Pressed felt face with painted features, brown eyes, painted lashes at upper right eye rims only, wistful expression, brunette mohair short curly wig, jointed at shoulders and hips. He wears one-piece grey felt pajamas with white edging and cuffs and pink buttons, and carries a plaid flannel blanket and handmade brown teddy bear made by Elaine Fujita-Gamble. The doll is marked on left foot, and has two original paper labels, one labeled "R. John Wright Babes in Toyland Timothy/No.1/50", and is contained in its original labeled box, with folded card labeled "Babes in Toyland, Timothy". The model was produced in 1983 only in an edition of 50. $1500/2200

6. Winnie the Pooh and His Favorite Chair

10". Of golden-ash mohair plush, the bear has swivel head and jointed limbs, tiny shoe-button eyes and black snout nose, and wears a jersey vest with pearl button. He stands alongside a green felt upholstered chair, and is contained in his original box shaped like a house. The bear has a cloth label on left foot, and his original paper wrist label with R.J.Wright signature. A leather tag on his back is numbered 240/500. Winnie was produced in edition of 500 exclusively for the Walt Disney World Doll and Teddy Bear Convention in Orlando in 1989. $1500/2000

"Within a year of creating that first doll John tried his hand at sculpting faces and these developed into his first molded felt dolls. He designed males and females, attired in costumes reminiscent of their homelands and appropriately accessorized. Because these dolls were handmade in a cottage industry setting, there were variations of clothing, colors, fabrics and shoes." (Shirley Bertrand, Characters of R. John Wright, page 7).

9. Guido, from Early Character Doll Series

17". Molded felt character features with wide beaming smile, brown eyes set into deep sockets, pronounced laughter crinkles, and cloth-sculpted ears. Guido is crowned with shaggy black hair and has a wide full moustache. He is jointed at shoulders and hips. Guido wears a print cotton shirt, mustard-yellow felt trousers, brown vest with gold buttons, black tie, burgundy felt cap, and black leather shoes. The doll has Wright stamp on its foot, and paper label with Vermont address, identifying the doll as "Guido". The model was produced from 1978-1981 only. $1000/1300

10. Holiday Winnie The Pooh

14". Of light brown mohair, firmly stuffed standing Winnie has swivel head, jointed shoulders with curved arms, very short jointed legs, black bead eyes, brown embroidered nose, open mouth. He is wearing black rubberized boots, a grey felt scarf with appliqué bands, and carries a bough of berries. Winnie has his original label "R. John Wright/Holiday Winnie the Pooh.928/1000", original certificate of authenticity, and is contained in his original labeled box along with an enamel pin from the 10th anniversary Walt Disney Bear and Doll Convention. Holiday Winnie the Pooh was produced for the 1997 10th Anniversary Disney convention in a numbered edition of 1000. $500/800

11. Bedtime Christopher Robin and Pooh

17 1/2". Of pressed felt with painted facial features, the brown-eyed boy has painted long curly upper lashes, rounded nose, solemn expression, brown mohair bobbed wig, swivel head, and jointed shoulders and hips. Christopher Robin is wearing striped cotton pajamas, blue felt slippers, maroon felt hooded bathrobe with cord edging, pockets, sash, and owns his own little Pooh bear of brown wool. He has original paper label "Christopher Robin and Pooh Bedtime/310/500" and gold button "RJW", original box with colorful illustration on the lid, and original certificate of authenticity. The set was produced in 1999 in a numbered edition of 500. $1400/1800

12. Rosa with Rolling Pin from Early Character Doll Series

17". Molded felt character features with wide beaming smile, brown side-glancing eyes set into deep sockets, tanned complexion, pronounced laughter crinkles, strong nose and high cheek bones. Rosa has thick graying brown hair pulled into a braided crown. She is jointed at shoulders and hips and wears a print calico blouse, long brown felt skirt, cotton apron, brown fringed shawl, petticoat, brown leggings, brown leather shoes and carries a wooden rolling pin. The doll has Wright stamp on its foot, and paper label with Vermont address, identifying the doll as "Rosa"; she is also lettered Rosa on her back. The model was produced in 1977 and 1978 only. $1500/2000

13. Rosa with Basket from Early Character Doll Series

17". Molded felt character features with wide beaming smile, brown side-glancing eyes set into deep sockets, tanned complexion, pronounced laughter crinkles, strong nose and high cheek bones. Rosa has thick graying brown hair pulled behind felt-sculpted ears into a coronet. She is jointed at shoulders and hips and wears a flowered green calico blouse, long black cotton skirt, checkered cotton apron, white dotted Swiss shawl, petticoat, orange leather shoes and carries a basket. The doll has Wright stamp on its foot, and paper label with Vermont address. The model was produced in 1977 and 1978 only. $1500/2000

14. Rachel – Sunday Best, Exclusive Model

18". A shy-faced girl with pressed felt facial features has brown eyes with upper painted lashes, solemn expression of lips, brunette mohair wig with bangs and pulled backward into ribbon at the crown, jointed arms and legs. She is wearing a dark teal velvet dress with lace edging, organdy petticoat and panties, brown leggings, black shoes, pearls, and carries a small felt doll with painted features and cotton dress and bonnet. The doll has Wright stamp on its foot, and two paper labels, one reading "R. John Wright/Rachel-Sunday Best/Made exclusively for Hobby Center Toys Bea Skydell's Toy Village/ No.94/250", and is contained in its original gold labeled box. The model was produced in 1985-1986 only in a numbered edition of 250. $1100/1500

15. The Little Prince, Prototype Model

18". Having pressed felt facial features with large dark brown eyes and painted lashes, plumper cheeks and rounded nose, the little boy has short blonde mohair curls, swivel head, jointed shoulders and hips. He is wearing a white aviation jump suit with yellow felt sash, silver medallions, grey felt boots, and a long bright green felt coat with brown felt lining and cuffs. Yellow felt cut-outs of stars decorate the shoulder epaulets, and the Prince holds an 8" stainless steel sword. The doll is hand-signed R. John Wright at back of head, and has an original paper label. The original silver box with The Little Prince label is hand-lettered "Artist Prototype/R.H. Wright". The doll based upon this prototype model was released in 1983-84 as an exclusive of 250 dolls for The Toy Shoppe. Included is a hand-written letter by the artist to the original owner of the doll. The doll was featured on the cover of *Characters of R. John Wright* by Shirley Bertrand. $3000/4000

16. The Little Prince, Centenary Edition

15". Having pressed felt facial features with unique sculpture, slender faced child with small painted eyes, nearly flattened nose, small mouth, blonde curly mohair wig, jointed shoulders and hips. He is wearing a white felt aviator jump suit with yellow felt sash, grey felt medallion and boots, dark green felt coat the brown lining and cuffs, yellow epaulet stars, silver sword. Original paper label "Centenary Edition the Little Prince, No.0256/1000, R.J. Wright...". The doll is included in a custom box with The Little Prince decorations and labels, and there is a certificate of authenticity. The model was released in 2000 in an edition of 1000. $800/1300

17. The Little Prince Aviator

15". Having pressed felt facial features with unique sculpture, slender shape of face, small painted eyes, nearly flattened nose, small mouth, blonde curly mohair wig, jointed shoulders and hips. He is wearing a lime green fitted felt

aviator jump suit with brown felt sash, grey slippers, yellow felt neck scarf, and owns a red felt rose that is posed on its own base. Original paper label "The Little Prince Aviator, No.037/250 R.J. Wright...". The doll is contained in a custom box with The Little Prince decorations and labels, and there is a certificate of authenticity. The model was released in 2002 in a numbered edition of 250. $700/1000

17A.The Fox from The Little Prince
5". Firmly stuffed shaded brown/red mohair fox has swivel head, four jointed legs, long fluffy tail, tiny bead eyes, felt lined ears in shaded pink colors. Original paper label "R. John Wright, The Fox, #196/250". The Fox is contained in its original box with an illustration of The Little Prince and The Fox, taken from drawings by St. Exupery; included is a certificate of authenticity. The model was released in 2002 in a numbered edition of 250. $300/350

18. Heidi and Snowflake, Exclusive Model

18". Having pressed felt facial features, small painted brown eyes, closed mouth with pensive soft expression, brunette mohair wig in short braids decorated with a coronet of edelweiss and mountain flowers, jointing at shoulders and hips. The doll is wearing a Tyrolean style costume with white blouse, embroidered velvet vest, maroon skirt, grey apron, petticoat, panties, grey woolen stockings, sturdy leather lace-up ankle boots, and is carrying her baby lamb Snowflake with swivel head. With original paper label "Heidi, #137/500 R. John Wright..." and with brass button "RJW". The doll is contained in its original custom box with illustration of the doll on its lid and has certificate of authenticity. The model was released in 2000 in a numbered edition of 500 for Little Switzerland Dolls of Huntington, New York. $1400/1800

19. Peter the Goatherd and Turk, Exclusive Model

18 1/2". Having pressed felt facial features whose pale blue eyes are enhanced by spiral threading, red and black upper eyeliner and side painted lashes, solemn expression on the pale lips of closed mouth, soft lambswool wig, jointing at shoulders and hips, bare feet with defined toes. He is wearing a green twill shirt with red tie, brown felt flannel lederhosen with suspenders and embroidery, green Tyrolean jacket with checkered cotton lining, grey hat with leather band, and carries a leather satchel with his lunch of bread and cheese. Included is his mohair Turk the goat with felt horns and hooves, leather collar, with original box. With original paper label "Peter the Goatherd #137/250 R. John Wright" and brass button "RJW". The doll is contained in its original custom box with illustration of the doll on its lid and has certificate of authenticity. The model was released in 2003 as an exclusive numbered edition of 250 dolls for Little Switzerland Dolls of Huntington, New York. $1500/1800

20. Giuseppe with Light Grey Beard, from Early Character Doll Series

17". Having pressed felt character features with wide beaming smile, broad nose, brown eyes set into deep sockets, pronounced laughter crinkles and mouth dimples, and cloth-sculpted ears. Giuseppe has a receding hairline, shaggy grey hair and a very long full grey beard. He is jointed at shoulders and hips. Giuseppe wears a plaid cotton shirt, khaki cotton trousers with black suspenders, wide brimmed black felt cap, and brown leather lace-up boots. He holds a three pronged pitchfork. The doll has Wright stamp on its foot. The model, appearing as F1 in early ads and known as Giuseppe, was produced in 1977 and 1978 only. $1400/1800

21. Giuseppe with Steel Grey Beard, from Early Character Doll Series

17". Having pressed felt character features with wide beaming smile, broad nose, brown eyes set into deep sockets, cloth-sculpted ears. Giuseppe has a receding hairline, shaggy grey hair and a full steel-grey beard. He is jointed at shoulders and hips. Giuseppe wears a green checkered cotton shirt, black flannel trousers with green suspenders, wide brimmed brown felt cap, and sienna leather lace-up boots. He holds a three pronged pitchfork. The doll has Wright stamp on its foot and paper label on wrist with Vermont address.. The model, appearing as F1 in early ads and known as Giuseppe, was produced in 1977 and 1978 only. $1400/1800

22. Giuseppe with Straw Hat, from Early Character Doll Series

17". Having pressed felt character features with wide beaming smile, broad nose, brown eyes set into deep sockets, impressed laughter crinkles below the eyes and at lip edges, cloth-sculpted ears. Giuseppe has a receding hairline, shaggy brown hair and a full brown beard with grey flecks. He is jointed at shoulders and hips. Giuseppe wears a green print cotton shirt, pale green flannel trousers with green suspenders, wide brimmed straw hat, and brown leather lace-up boots. He holds a three pronged pitchfork. The doll has Wright stamp on its foot and paper label on wrist with Vermont address. The model, appearing as F1 in early ads and known as Giuseppe, was produced in 1977 and 1978 only. $1400/1800

20. Close-up.

22B. Acorn Napkin Ring
5"w. With circular felt-covered ring, the decorative novelty is ornamented with autumn-tinted cut-out leaves and two felt acorns. The novelty was presented as a party favor at a UFDC convention. $200/300

23. Hannah from Little Children Series I
16". Having pressed felt swivel head with well-defined facial sculpting especially around the eyes and chin, painted brown eyes with dark eyeliner, rounded nose, closed mouth, blonde mohair wig in soft curls with tiny braids clasped at back of head felt body with jointing at shoulders and hips, wearing brown plaid dress of fine lightweight wool, ruffled bretelles, petticoat, pantalets, wool stockings, leather ankle boots, with original paer label "Little Children Series I Hannah, #5/250" and original green paper label on front of dress. The doll has her original box and NIADA certificate of authenticity. Hannah was made in an edition of 250, of which this is #5, an early issue, between 1981-1985. $1200/1500

24. MacTavish with Green Beret, from Early Character Doll Series
17". Having pressed felt character features with hand-painted wide beaming smile, prominent nose, brown eyes set into deep sockets, impressed laughter crinkles around the eyes, cloth-sculpted ears. MacTavish has cropped blonde-grey hair and neatly trimmed matching beard. He is jointed at shoulders and hips, and wears a tan felt shirt with button flap at the front, black cuffs and waist, sienna corduroy trousers, brown leather shoes, plaid woolen scarf, and green felt large beret with cream pom-pom. He carries an applewood walking stick. The doll has Wright stamp on its foot and paper booklet on wrist with Vermont address and is hand-lettered "MacTavish". The model, was produced from 1979 to 1981 only. $1200/1500

24A. Jenny from Early Character Doll Series
17". Having pressed felt character features on swivel head, large brown painted eyes, broad nose, wide gentle smile, wheat blonde hair drawn into a braid at the back of head, five piece felt body, wearing olive green felt jacket with brown felt edging, gold buttons, plaid homespun skirt, woven tweed head scarf, petticoat, pantalets, brown stockings, brown leather shoes, carrying walking stick. The doll has Wright stamp on its foot and original wrist booklet indicating "Jenny". The doll was made from 1979-1981. $1200/1500

25. Lifesize Winnie the Pooh

18". Of shaved light brown mohair, plump-bellied Winnie is firmly stuffed, has swivel head, jointed limbs with curve-shaped left arm, glass eyes, and is wearing a knit vest with one button. The bear has original labeled box and two original paper hang-tags, identifying him as No.1467 from the numbered edition of 2500. The bear, licensed by Disney, was issued in 1987-88. $500/800

26. Kanga and Roo from Winnie the Pooh Premiere Series

9". Of dark brown wool plush with white under-side, Kanga has glass eyes, stand-up ears, jointed legs, and a pouch for holding Roo. With original box, and original hang tag identifying the pair as #806 from the numbered edition of 1000 issued in 1985-1987, and with RJW brass button. $400/500

27. Winnie the Pooh from the Premiere Series

8". Of light brown wool plush the chubby-torso bear with short legs and curved left arm has swivel head and jointed limbs, shoe-button bead eyes, and wears a knit burgundy one-button vest. With original box and original hang tag identifying Winnie as #1095 from a numbered edition of 2500. The series was issued in 1985-1987. $400/500

28. Piglet from Winnie the Pooh Premiere Series

5". Of tinted pink felt the standing piglet has jointed arms and legs, bead eyes, and wears a green knitted suit. With original box and original hand tag identifying Piglet as #591 from a numbered edition of 1000. The series was issued in 1985-1987. $400/500

29. Tigger from Winnie the Pooh Premiere Series

6"l. Of shaved wool plush with painted tiger stripes, Tigger has swivel head, jointed legs, curvy tail, glass eyes, whiskers. With original box and original seam cloth tag. Tigger is from the 1985-1987 premiere numbered edition of 1000. $400/500

30. Eeyore from Winnie the Pooh Premiere Series

10"l. Of shaved brown wool, with very plump torso, jointed neck with long floppy ears, jointed legs with plump back legs, tail with black fringe. With original box and original cloth seam tag and paper hanging tag identifying Eeyone as #764 from the premiere numbered series of 1000. Eeyore was issued in 1985-1987. $400/600

31. Lifesize Piglet

9". Of tinted pink felt the standing piglet has swivel head with upturned nose, black bead eyes, jointed limbs, plump tummy, and wears a green knit suit. With original box and original cloth seam tag, and paper tag identifying Piglet as #887 from a numbered edition of 1000. Piglet was issued in 1987. $400/600

32. Christopher Robin and Winnie the Pooh from Series I

18". Having pressed felt character face with painted brown eyes in deeply set eye sockets, eye outlined and side painted lashes, closed mouth with full lips, short brunette bobbed mohair wig, jointed shoulders and hips. He is wearing a blue cotton smock with pockets over white shirt and brown shorts with suspenders, brown leather shoes, white cotton cap. The doll has original metal pin, and original paper label "Christopher Robin and Winnie the Pooh, No 150/1000 R. John Wright" and is contained, along with matching Winnie the Pooh bear, in original box with illustration on the label, and includes an autographed note from the artist The pair was of the 1985-1987 Series I set of Winnie the Pooh, under license from Disney. The doll and bear are featured on the cover of *Characters of R. John Wright* by Shirley Bertrand. $2200/2800

33. Theo from Bear Lodge

15". Slender boy with pressed felt character face, small painted blue eyes, black upper eyeliner, closed mouth with pale lips, blonde mohair fleecy wig, jointed shoulders and hips. Theo is wearing a felt taupe jacket with pockets and self-covered buttons, brown felt shorts, black woolen knee socks, brown leather hiking boots, straw hat with leather band, brown felt scarf discreetly embroidered UFDC, and carries a walking stick and mohair covered backpack with two brass RJW pins, and enclosing a green woolen blanket. The doll has original paper label "Bear Lodge-Theo, #7/100, R. John Wright" and is contained with original labeled box with certificate of authenticity. Theo was released at 2002 UFDC convention in a numbered edition of 100. $900/1100

34. Scout from Bear Lodge

9". Of short smoke-grey tinted mohair with shaved detail around the eyes and muzzle, the standing bear has black bead eyes, stitched smiling mouth, swivel head, jointed limbs, felt paws, resin claws, and wears felt scarf embroidered UFDC. Scout has original paper label "Bear Lodge Scout UFDC Denver 2002 R. John Wright", and is contained in original labeled cylinder box, autographed by R. John Wright. Scout was presented at 2002 UFDC convention in an exclusive edition of 250. $300/400

35. Max and His Pinocchio

17". Having pressed felt face with pale grey-green eyes, closed mouth with solemn expression, dark brown bobbed wig, swivel head, jointed shoulders and hips. Max is wearing a white long-sleeved shirt with pearl buttons, grey felt lederhosen with green felt edging, suspenders, embroidered detail, white stockings, brown strap shoes, green felt Tyrolean hat, and carries a wooden Pinocchio with jointed limbs and painted costume, gilt letterer "Geppeto's Toys" on its chest. The doll has original paper label "Max and his Pinocchio, made exclusively for Geppetto's Toys, Boston/New York, #66/150" and is stamped on its foot. Max is contained in original red box with paper label and includes an autographed note from R. John Wright along with a certificate of registration. $1500/2000

36. Wooden Pinocchio, Artist Proof

9". Carved alpine-maple wooden figure has sculpted and painted facial features, side-glancing eyes, black mohair wig, dowel-articulation at shoulders, elbows, hips and knees, sculpted large white gloved hands, large feet with brown strap shoes, wearing felt costume of white shirt, black vest, red shorts, yellow felt hat, with blue bow tie, carrying Pinocchio booklet . The figure is hand-signed R.J. Wright and Susan Wright on the feet, and inscribed "AP 4/5"; there is a brass RJW button. Pinocchio is contained in his original box noted "artist proof 4". The doll was issued in 1994 in an edition of 250 with this style eyes although this is prototype, 4/5. $800/1000

37. Geppetto and Pinocchio

18" Geppetto. Geppetto having pressed felt character face portraying older gentle man, O-shaped down-glancing eyes, large red nose, impressed cheek and brow crinkles, white mohair wig and bushy moustache, swivel head, jointed arms and legs, individually sculpted fingers, posed in slightly arthritic manner, wearing pale lavender felt shirt, black trousers, green suspenders, embroidered bib, brown vest with tan lining, green knit leggings, brown leather buckle shoes, booklet and wearing spectacles. He is stamped on his foot and has original paper label "Walt Disney's Geppetto & Pinocchio, Series II Traditional, #75/250" Pinocchio, 9", is all alpine-maple wooden with painted features, side-glancing animated eyes, brown mohair wig, cloth costume, tan Tyrolean hat with red felt feather, fully articulated, and hand-lettered 75/250 on his foot along with RJW brass button. The two dolls are presented in their original labeled box along with certificate of authenticity. The set was released in 1994 in an edition of 250. $1800/2300

38. Geppetto's Chair

9 1/2". Of alpine-maple carved wood with outlined seat, fancy heart-shaped carving on back and sturdy legs. The chair is hand-lettered 75/500 with RJW brass button. The chair was made for R. John Wright by Anri of Italy on special commission, based upon Wright's original carving inspired by the Disney Pinocchio movie, and was released in 1992 in a numbered edition of 500. $200/300

39. Pleasure Island Pinocchio with Felt Ears and Tail

9". Of alpine-maple carved wood with painted features, side-glancing animated eyes, dark mohair wig, dowel-jointing at shoulders, elbows, hips and knees, sculpted large white-gloved hands and feet with brown shoes, original felt costume based upon the rendition of Pinocchio in the Disney film; however this Pinocchio also has a long brown felt tail, and long felt ears. The doll is autographed and dated on its right foot, numbered 101/250 with brass RJW button on its right foot, has original booklet, and is contained in its original labeled red box with certificate of authenticity, and an enamel button from 1992 Disneyana convention. This model of Pinocchio was an exclusive numbered edition for that convention. $500/700

40. Geppetto Searches for Pinocchio

18". Of pressed felt with character face portraying an older man, O-shaped down-glancing eyes, large red-tipped nose, impressed wrinkles on cheeks and forehead, white mohair wig and bushy beard, felt-sculpted ears, jointed shoulders and hips, wire armature at knees, and wearing grey felt shirt, black short trousers with suspenders and embroidered bib, grey felt fringed scarf, brown felt lined coat, orange felt stocking cap with white pom-pom, knit stockings, brown leather buckle shoes, wearing spectacles and carrying a lantern and booklet. Geppetto is stamped on foot and has original paper label "Geppetto Searches for Pinocchio, #98/250, R. John Wright" and RJW brass button. He is contained in his original labeled box with certificate of authenticity. This model was released in 1996 in a 250 numbered edition. $1100/1300

**41. Mario with Plaid Pants and Cigar,
from Early Character Doll Series**

17". Having pressed felt character features with wide beaming smile, broad nose bridge, brown side-glancing eyes set into deep sockets, deep crinkles under the eyes, cloth-sculpted ears. Mario has black hair with long sideburns and a full black moustache. He is jointed at shoulders and hips, and wears a white dotted cotton shirt, plaid trousers, maroon felt vest with silver buttons, brown brimmed cap and black leather shoes. He holds a cigar. The doll has Wright stamp on its foot and paper label on wrist with Vermont address, hand-lettered "Mario". The model appeared as A1 in early ads and was produced in 1977 and 1978 only. $1200/1500

42. Bernard with Plaid Shirt from Early Character Doll Series

17". Having pressed felt character features with wide beaming smile, broad nose bridge, brown painted eyes set into deep sockets, thick black upper eyeliner, deep crinkles under the eyes, cloth-sculpted ears. Bernard has brown side-parted hair with uneven sideburns and bangs brushed across his forehead. He is jointed at shoulders and hips, and wears a plaid flannel smock, orange felt short pants, brown woolen stockings, leather clogs with wooden soles, yellow cotton scarf, and carries a woven harvest basket on his back. The doll has Wright stamp on its foot and paper label on wrist with Vermont address, NIADA designation, and labeled "Bernard". The model was released in 1979-1981 only. $1200/1500

43. Old Man with Stick from Early Character Doll Series

17". Having pressed felt features with gentle expression, brown eyes set into deeply sculpted sockets, laughter crinkles around the eyes, broad bridge of nose, wide smile, sculpted ears, grey/golden long hair with receding hairline at forehead, long wavy beard, jointing at shoulders and hips. He wears a plaid cotton shirt, corduroy sienna trousers, tan felt vest with snaps, brown shoes, long woolen scarf, and blue felt beret with white woolen pom-pom, and carries a two-pronged stick. The doll is stamped on his foot and has Vermont hang tag. This was the first character doll model, and appeared in early advertisements as L1. The doll was offered in 1977 and 1978. $1200/1500

44. Karl from Early Character Doll Series

17". Having pressed felt character features, broad nose bridge, blue painted eyes set into deep sockets, thick black upper eyeliner, deep crinkles under the eyes, cloth-sculpted ears. Karl has tousled brown mohair wig and very bushy brown moustache. He is jointed at shoulders and hips, and wears a burgundy felt jacket with green wide cuffs and wide lapels over brown shirt, black shorts, silk tie, woolen leggings, brown leather shoes, and green felt Tyrolean hat with felt appliqué trim; he carries a gnarled apple-wood walking stick. The doll has Wright stamp on its foot and paper label on wrist with Vermont address and labeled "Karl". The model was released in 1979-1981 only. $1200/1500

45. Nighttime Winnie the Pooh

12". Of light tan soft mohair that is firmly stuffed, Willie has black glass eyes, brown embroidered nose, very chubby torso with shortened legs, jointed arms and legs, curved right arm. He is wearing a cream knit nightshirt and stockinette cap, and carries a tin candlestick with snuffer. He wears blue felt slippers and owns a maroon felt package with extra candles. He has original label "R. John Wright Nighttime Winnie the Pooh, #359/2500" and is contained in original labeled box with certificate of authenticity. The bear was released in 1998 in an edition of 2500 although only 1537 bears were made. $500/700

45A. Bear's Bed

15"l. Painted white iron spindled bed with ball finials is fitted with old-fashioned mattress, and covered with an assortment of linens, pillow and wool flannel blankets. The bed has original paper label "Bear's Bed, #3/500, R. John Wright" and is contained in it original labeled box with certificate of authenticity. The bed was released in 1999 in a numbered edition of 500. $200/300

46. Winnie the Pooh with Bee

14". Light brown mohair bear is firmly stuffed, has rounded head with upturned snout, black embroidered nose tip, black glass eyes, very plump torso, jointed short legs, jointed arms with curved left arm. Winnie has a felt-winged bee attached to his right ear and wears a white towel bib; the original "hunny pot" is missing. He is labeled with a wooden button marked "R. John Wright Inc. Toys #234/5000" and is contained in his (worn) original box without name label but with colorful illustration on the lid. The bear was released in 1987-1989 in a numbered edition of 5000. $500/700

47. Winnie the Pooh and His Favorite Chair

10". Of golden-ash mohair plush, the bear has swivel head and jointed limbs, tiny shoe-button eyes and black snout nose. He owns a green felt upholstered chair, and is contained in his original box shaped like a house. Winnie is missing his jersey vest and there is a small moth hole in the chair. The bear has a cloth label on left foot, and his original paper wrist label with R.J.Wright signature. A leather tag on his back is numbered 19/500. Winnie was produced in edition of 500 exclusively for the Walt Disney World Doll and Teddy Bear Convention in Orlando in 1989. $1800/2200

48. Little Red Riding Hood, Artist Proof

20". Having pressed felt face with painted features, brown side-glancing eyes, fringed brows, closed mouth with very fretful expression, very dark long curly mohair wig, jointing at shoulders and hips. She is wearing a white cotton blouse and brown felt skirt with black edging, white dimity apron, ruffled petticoat and pantalets, grey woolen knit leggings, cordovan leather shoes with brass buckle, and a red felt hooded cape with white lining. She carries a woven basket that contains lunch: bread, pear, wedge of cheese and a miniature box of tea with amusing R. John Wright label and the note "guaranteed to soothe the stomach after over-eating". There is an original label on the skirt "R. John Wright, Little Red Riding Hood, AP5/500" and a hang tag autographed by the artist. The doll is contained in its original box labeled "AP5/500". The doll was an original artist proof. The model was released from 1988-1991 is a numbered edition of 500. $1000/1400

49. Gollibaby Boy and Girl, Collectors Club Editions

5". Each is of black pressed felt with painted facial features, googly eyes painted to be glancing at each other, coral lips, mohair curl at forehead, jointed baby arms and legs. Boy is wearing a cream felt diaper with green and yellow appliqués, matching bib and large yellow felt beret; he holds a felt striped ball. Girl is wearing a green felt diaper with white appliqué polka dots, matching bib and bonnet with white ruffles and is holding a toy felt duckling. Each has original paper label on back "R. John Wright, GolliBaby Boy (or Girl) #22", and the pair is contained in original labeled box with certificates of authenticity. They were produced exclusively for the R. John Wright Collectors Club in 2000/2001. Only 320 sets were made. $600/900

50. Sunshine Scootles, Collectors Club Edition

6 1/2". Having pressed felt head with unusual sculpted hair, forelock curl, painted blue side-glancing eyes, swivel head, jointed arms and legs. The doll is wearing a sunshine yellow cotton dress with white rick-rack, matching bloomers, white shoes and socks, yellow hair and wrist bands, and carries two white felt flowers with yellow centers and long green stems. There is a brass RJW button on back of doll, and she is contained in her original box with certificate of authenticity indicating that Sunshine Scootles is #348 from a 2004/2005 edition available to Wright Collectors Club members only. $400/500

51. Fleur Flower Kewpie. UFDC Exclusive

6". Having pressed felt head with classic Kewpie features, painted side-glancing eyes, blue felt wings, jointed arms and legs. Kewpie is wearing a petal style dress of green and shaded pink felt with gathered ribbon skirt, and an affixed felt cap in the shape of an upside down petal with stem on the top. There is an original paper label "Fleur, #205/250, Made for the United Federation of Doll Clubs 1999" that is autographed by R. John Wright and an RJW brass button. The doll is contained in its original box with certificate of authenticity and notation that the doll was made exclusively for the 50th anniversary of UFDC in 1999 in an edition of 250 dolls. $700/1000

52. Kewpie and Teddy, Collectors Club Edition

6". Having pressed felt head with classic Kewpie features, sculpted topknot curl, painted side-glancing eyes, blue felt wings, jointed limbs. Kewpie wears only a large green felt sailor's cap with black silk banding labeled RJW Club, and carries a 2 1/2" brown jointed teddy bear with swivel head and jointed limbs. There is a red paper heart on Kewpie's chest and a paper label on back "Kewpie & Teddy, #203". Both Kewpie and Teddy have RJW brass buttons, and they are contained in original labeled box with certificate of authenticity. The set was released in 1999/2000 exclusively for members of the R. John Wright Collectors Club; only 520 sets were produced. $400/600

53. Miss Golli, Collectors Club Edition

11". Having black pressed felt face with large O-shaped upper glancing googly eyes, widely smiling red felt lips, black fleecy hair, jointed shoulders and hips. Miss Golli is wearing red felt gown with yellow felt appliqué dots, white scalloped collar and cuffs, green felt sash and reticule, yellow felt sunbonnet with green streamers, petticoat, pantalets, stockings, black leather shoes. She has original paper label "R. John Wright's Miss Golli, #530/2500" (a matched number to Golliwogg below) and is contained in original box with

certificate of authenticity. Miss Golli was released in 1997, the second model created exclusively for the Wright Collector's Club. Although the edition was limited to 2500, only 849 models were made. $500/750

54. Golliwogg, The First Collector's Club Edition

11". Having black pressed felt face with large O-shaped side-glancing googly eyes, widely smiling white felt lips, black fleecy hair, jointed shoulders and hips. Golliwog is wearing red felt vest, green felt jacket with long tails, black white checkered felt pants, yellow felt bow tie and stockings, white gloves, brown leather buckle shoes. He has original paper label "R. John Wright's Golliwog, #530/2500" (a matched number to Miss Golli, above) and is contained in original box with certificate of authenticity. Golliwog was released in 1996, and is the premiere model of Wright Collector's Club dolls. Although the edition was limited to 2500, only 1526 models were made. $500/750

55. Periwinkle, the R. John Wright Trademark, Prototype with Center-Seam Face

7". Of felt, constructed with sewn center-seam face and painted features, squinting eyes, stitched ears, green felt elf cap, pale green felt body with jointed arms and legs, white felt collar and silver buttons, grey stiffened-organdy wings with embroidered detail, hanging loop. Periwinkle has original R. John Wright Vermont-address paper label, and was one of only two prototype sewn-face models released in August, 1980. $1000/1500

56. Periwinkle, Wright Trademark Doll with Flower

7". Of pressed felt with swivel head, artfully painted facial features, elf ears, green felt cap, pale green felt body with jointed shoulders and hips, white felt collar and cuffs, silver buttons, stiffened organdy wings with embroidery, hanging loop, and holding red felt flower with green stem. Periwinkle has original R. John Wright Vermont-address label and booklet, NIADA certificate, and pencil note "PW-56". The figure was released in 1981 and produced in very limited number. $1000/1500

57. Teddy Bear, Collector Club Edition

9". Of shaved brown mohair the swivel head bear is firmly stuffed, with glass side-glancing eyes, embroidered nose, jointed elongated arms, hip-jointed short legs, felt paws, stitched claws, with red neck bow and brass Periwinkle stick pin. He has original label "R. John Wright's Teddy Bear, #530/2500", original box and certificate of authenticity, and RJW brass button. Teddy Bear was made in 1996, exclusively available to Collector Club members; only 866 examples were produced. $300/500

58. Periwinkle Pincushion, Collector Club Edition

6" seated. Of pressed felt with swivel head, artfully painted facial features, elf ears, green felt cap, pale green felt body with jointed shoulders and hips, white felt collar and cuffs, silver buttons, grey felt wings with embroidery, hanging loop, cupped hands, Periwinkle is seated upon a red felt pincushion and holds a threaded needle. Periwinkle has original label "R. John Wright Periwinkle, #356", original box, and certificate of authenticity. The model was released in 1998 as a Collector club exclusive; 807 examples were produced. $350/500

59. Hummingbird

4". Of mohair with shaded green/purple/cream coloring, painted felt wings, black bead eyes, metal beak and feet. Hummingbird has original brass RJW button, and is contained in original box with certificate of authenticity, indicating #313/500, and 2004 release date. $200/300

60. Peter, from Little Children Series I

17". Having pressed felt face with painted features, grey eyes, painted upper side lashes, blonde curly mohair wig, jointing at shoulders and hips. Peter wears white cotton shirt, brown five-button vest, green felt shorts with side pockets, green thick woolen stockings, black leather shoes with brown straps and carries a cotton plaid knapsack with leather straps containing toy cheese and bread. He has original Periwinkle green/gold label, original paper label "R. John Wright, Little Children, Series I, Peter, #58/250", and is contained in original labeled box. He was produced from 1981-1985 in a limited numbered series of 250. $1100/1500

61. Erica from Early Character Doll Series

17". Having pressed felt character features, pointy nose, brown
painted eyes set into deep sockets, thick black upper eyeliner, grey
lower eyeliner. Erica has brown mohair wig in tight coiled braids at
side of head. She is jointed at shoulders and hips, and wears a white
cotton blouse, green felt gown with brown laced sash, cotton apron,
blue shawl, petticoat, pantalets, stockings, black felt shoes, grey felt
hat with flowers. The doll has Wright stamp on its foot, paper label
on wrist with Vermont address, paper label on skirt labeled EZ-17.
The model, marketed as Erica, was released in 1979-1981 only.
$1100/1500

62. Tickles from Baby Bear Collection, Exclusive Edition

12". Of soft brown shaved mohair with glass eyes, resin noise, open
mouth with felt tongue, plump torso, jointed baby arms and legs in
curved pose, felt paws with painted detail, resin claws, holding a
cluster of green felt leaves and berries. Tickles has original RJW
button and paper label "R. John Wright Baby Bear Collection,
Tickles, Made for the Toy Shoppe, #65/500", certificate of
authenticity and original labeled box. Tickles was released in 2000
in an exclusive edition of 500 for the Toy Shoppe. $450/650

63. Pep from the Baby Bear Collection, Exclusive Edition

12". Of soft steel-black mohair plush with shaded color around the muzzle and white mohair beard, Pep has rounded face and torso, short curved baby arms and legs, glass eyes, resin nose and paws, felt tongue and paws with detailed painting, holding a felt branch of leaves and acorns. Pep has original brass RJW button, original paper label "R. John Wright Pep #65/500", original box with certificate of authenticity and booklet. The model was an exclusive for Village Bears and Collectibles The Toy Shoppe, the fourth in the Baby Bear collection, and was released in 2000 in a numbered edition of 500. $450/650

64. Gretchen from Early Character Doll Series

17". Having pressed felt character features, pointy nose, brown painted eyes set into deep sockets, thick black upper eyeliner, grey lower eyeliner. Gretchen has brown mohair wig in long braids. She is jointed at shoulders and hips, and wears a white dotted cotton blouse, green felt skirt, brown felt vest, tan apron, shawl, petticoat, brown woolen leggings, black felt shoes with pom-poms, black felt cap with cutouts and scalloped edging, and carries a wooden crook trimmed with felt flowers. The doll has Wright stamp on its foot, paper label on wrist with Vermont address and name "Gretchen" and NIADA certificate indicating the doll is "Gretchen, Swiss Shepheress", model G-2, and was produced in 1981, #14/250. $1100/1500

65. Paddington Bear

15". Brown mohair firmly stuffed bear with round chubby face and torso, black mohair ears, resin nose, black glass eyes, jointed limbs, curved right paw, felt paws, wearing blue felt duffle coat with toggle buttons, red lining in hood, black felt hat, carrying brown leather valise, original label "Please look after this bear. Thank you." With original paper label "R. John Wright Paddington Bear, #859/2500", and contained in original labeled box with certificate of authenticity and booklet. The bear was released in 2000. $500/600

66. Party Tigger

3 1/2". Of shaved mohair plush in tan color with painted brown striped, armature-shaped long curly tail, black bead eyes, jointed limbs, wearing a grey party hat with white pleats and orange polka dots. With original RJW brass button, cloth label, paper booklet with story, and contained in original labeled box with certificate of authenticity indicating #3472/3500. Party Tigger was issued in 1996. $300/400

67. Piglet with Violets

8". Of pink velvet with center seam face, shaped nose, blushed painted detail, black glass eyes, stitched ears, jointed arms, wearing green jersey and holding a handful of felt long-stemmed violets. With original cloth label, brass RJW button, wooden button "Classic Winnie the Pooh, #1384/2500", and contained in original labeled box. The edition was produced under license to Walt Disney in 1988. $400/600

68. Pocket Pooh Collection, Matched Set of Eight

2 3/4" – 11". Including Christopher Robin in pressed felt wearing blue smock, along with seven mohair animals from Winnie the Pooh stories. Each animal is fully jointed, and all are labeled with original brass pin, cloth tags, booklets, and contained in original numbered boxes. The Pooh pocket dolls were issued in 1998-1999, and this is a matched set, each numbered 1910/3500. $3000/3500

69. Geppetto and Pinocchio, Series I, Marionettes

9" and 18". Including pressed felt Geppetto with down-glancing O'shaped painted eyes, long pointy nose with red tip, white mohair hair and bushy beard, impressed age wrinkles, jointed arms and legs, wearing felt costume, leather buckle shoes, and holding marionette strings that are attached to carved alpine maple wood Pinocchio with "O" shaped eyes, felt costume, painted shoes and gloves. Pinocchio has RJW brass button, and marked 75/500 on foot. Geppetto has original RJW brass button, and paper label "Geppetto & Pinocchio Series I Marionette #75/500. The pair is contained in original labeled box with certificates of authenticity. They were released in 1994-1995 in a numbered edition of 500. $2000/2500

70. Lillian and Arthur, Little Sister, Little Brother Series

18" and 20". Each is of pressed felt with painted facial fetures, the boy with chubbier face and blonde mohair wig, the girl with more slender older face and auburn mohair wig, painted brows eyes, stitched ears, closed mouth, jointed arms and legs. The girl wears blue cotton sailor dress, petticoat, pantalets, white stockings, black strap shoes, and carries a jump rope. The boy wears white middy shirt and sailor cap, green felt shorts, red woolen stockings, white shoes and carries a toy boat. Each has brass RJW button and paper label indicating "Arthur (or Lillian) R John Wright #87/500". They are contained together in double labeled box indicating the dolls were an exclusive edition for The Toy Shoppe, The Enchanted Doll, and Hobby Center Toys. The set was produced in 1987-89 in a number edition of 500. $1600/2000

R. John and Susan Wright first introduced child dolls in 1981 in their series named Little Children, and, in fact, the original production drawing for the 1981 series was named Lillian. However, it was not until 1987-1989 that a doll named Lillian was actually created in another series named Childhood Classics. She was the 20" big sister of 18" Arthur, and she had an entirely different facial sculpt than the dolls of the original Little Children Series. Production was very limited, and only four other dolls with this facial model were ever issued, Patrick and his Bear (250 dolls), Hans and Gretel Brinker (350 dolls each, #1 and 2 in this book) and Little Red Riding Hood (500 dolls, #48 in this book).

71. Luna Kewpie

6". Dark brown pressed felt Kewpie with black side-glancing eyes, swivel head, jointed limbs, large stiffened green felt wings with painted butterfly decorations, white wool cap and suit, leaf ears. With RJW brass buttons and original label "Luna, R. John Wright #239/250". In original box with certificate of authenticity. Luna was released in 2001 in a numbered edition of 250. $500/700

72. Flit Kewpie, Exclusive

6". Pressed felt kewpie with dark side-glancing eyes, swivel head, jointed arms and legs, appliquéd brown skullcap with topknot, antennae, green felt suit, ladybug wings with painted decorations, blue wings, holding felt flower. With RJW brass button and original label "Flit, R. John Wright #205/250". In original box with certificate of authenticity. Flit was released in 1999 in a numbered edition 250 exclusively for UFDC 50th anniversary. $800/1100

73. Caper Kewpie Bug

6". Pressed felt Kewpie with black side-glancing eyes, swivel head, jointed limbs, two tone grey felt wings with organdy overlay, blue wings, green felt fitted cap and matching suit with dark green felt buttons, holding purple flower. With RJW brass buttons and original label "Caper, R. John Wright #208/250". In original box with certificate of authenticity. Caper was released in 2001 in a numbered edition of 250. $500/700

74. Crocus Flower Kewpie

6". Pressed felt Kewpie with black side-glancing eyes, swivel head, jointed limbs, blue wings, purple petal-shaped cap with stem, purple tunic with scalloped floral-shaped skirt, green felt lower body and legs, yellow petals on feet, purple silk ruffled sleeves. . With RJW brass buttons and original label "Caper, R. John Wright #208/250". In original box with certificate of authenticity. Crocus was released in 2001 in a numbered edition of 250. $500/700

75. Large Wooden Pinocchio, Disneyland Exclusive

16". Of carved alpine maple wood with painted side-glancing O-shaped eyes, long pointy nose, black mohair wig, jointing at shoulders, elbows, hips and knees, painted large white gloves and over-sized brown shoes. Wearing felt white shirt, black vest, red shorts with felt appliqué designs at the side, felt yellow Tyrolean hat. With brass RJW button, paper label "R. John Wright Disney Collection Pinocchio #9/500" and with booklet and original labeled box and certificate of authenticity. This model of Pinocchio was released in 2000 in a numbered edition of 500, made exclusively for Disneyland. $1000/1500

76. Mickey Mouse, Disneyland Exclusive

12". Of pressed felt with white mask face, O-shaped black eyes, black nose, wide smile with felt tongue, black felt fears and body, red felt pants with white buttons, white gloved hands, yellow felt feet. With original paper label "R. John Wright, The Disney Collection, Mickey Mouse #277/500", wrist booklet, enamel pin from 2005 Walt Disney World Teddy Bear and Doll Weekend, and contained in original labeled box with certificate of authenticity. The model was released in 2005 in a numbered edition of 500 exclusively for the Disney World convention. $500/700

77. Hottentot Kewpie

6". Dark brown pressed felt Kewpie with black side-glancing eyes, swivel head, jointed limbs, blue wings, red heart label on chest. With RJW brass buttons and original label "Hottentot R. John Wright #115/500". In original box with certificate of authenticity. Hottentot was released in 2001 in a numbered edition of 250. $500/700

78. Peeper Kewpie

6". Pressed felt Kewpie with black side-glancing eyes, swivel head, jointed limbs, blue wings, shaded brown bug body with brown legs, wearing navy blue skull cap with antennae, navy blue long coat with tails, green spats, green silk bow tie. With RJW brass buttons and original label "Peeper, R. John Wright #106/250". In original box with certificate of authenticity. Peeper was released in 2001 in a numbered edition of 250. $500/700

79. Poppy Flower Kewpie

6". Pressed felt Kewpie with black side-glancing eyes, swivel head, jointed limbs, blue wings, with green felt headband decorated with felt flowers, poppy-shaped dress with orange silk underskirt. With RJW brass buttons and original label "Peeper, R. John Wright #208/250". In original box with certificate of authenticity. Poppy was released in 2001 in a numbered edition of 250. $500/700

80. Lulu Kewpie

6". Dark brown pressed felt Kewpie with black side-glancing eyes, swivel head, jointed limbs, blue wings, white felt petals framing the face, yellow centers, green and dark green felt petal dress, stiffened organdy green petal tip on head. With RJW brass buttons and original label "Lulu, R. John Wright #106/250". In original box with certificate of authenticity. Lulu was released in 2001 in a numbered edition of 250. $500/700

81. Raggedy Ann, Premier Edition
18". Firmly pressed ball-shaped felt head with painted complexion and facial features, black wooden bead eyes, applied diamond-shaped nose, red yarn hair, swivel head, jointing at shoulders, hips and knees, wearing blue felt dress with appliqué flowers, white cotton pinafore and pantalets, striped stockings, black felt shoes. The doll has original label "Premier Edition Raggedy Ann 313/1000" and is contained in original deluxe box with certificate of authenticity. The doll was released in 2004. $600/900

82. Raggedy Andy, Premier Edition
18". Firmly pressed ball-shaped felt head with painted complexion and facial features, black wooden bead eyes, applied diamond-shaped nose, red yarn hair, swivel head, jointing at shoulders, hips and knees, wearing blue felt pants and white felt shirt with felt appliqué stripes, blue felt cap, black bow. The doll has original label "Premier Edition Raggedy Andy 313/1000" and is contained in original deluxe box with certificate of authenticity. The doll was released in 2004. $600/900

83. Raggedy Ann, The Magical Hour
9". Firmly pressed ball-shaped felt head with painted complexion and facial features, black wooden bead eyes, applied diamond-shaped nose, brown yarn hair, swivel head, jointing at shoulders, hips and knees, wearing white cotton dress, white cotton pantalets, striped stockings, black felt shoes, carrying felt heart-shaped pillow embroidered "Love one another". The doll has original label "Raggedy Ann, The Magical Hour,204/400", brass RJW button, and is contained in original deluxe box with certificate of authenticity. The doll was released in 2004. $400/600

84. Raggedy Ann Wooden Bed
10"l. Painted forest green wooden bed with cannon-ball posts is fitted with sheet, pillow and white felt black with appliqué patches. Authographed by R. John Wright on bottom of bed slat and stamped RJW. Contained in original labeled box and designed as an accompaniment to Raggedy Ann, The Magical Hour. $300/350

85. Scott from Little Children Series
17". Pressed felt character head with painted facial features, light brown eyes, reddish blonde curly tousled hair, jointing at shoulders and hips. Scott is wearing knitted woolen argyle sweater, white cotton shirt, grey felt shorts, magenta woolen knit cap, white knit stockings, and laced leather shoes, (original school bag is missing). He has brass RJW button back and original label "R. John Wright Little Children Series II, #220/250", and is contained in his original labeled box. $900/1200

86. Old Lady with Rake Early Character Doll Series

17". Pressed felt character features, pointy nose, brown painted eyes set into deep sockets, thick black upper eyeliner, brown mohair wig in bun at nape of neck, swivel head, jointing at shoulders and hips. She wears a (faded) striped dress with white sleeves and attached pinafore, petticoat, linen-like head scarf, and carries a wooden rake. The doll has Wright stamp on its foot, paper label on wrist with Vermont address. She appeared in the first R. John Wright advertisement described as model B2. The doll was made in 1977-1978. $1100/1500

87. Nippy from the Baby Bear Collection, Exclusive Edition

12". Of white mohair plush, Nippy has rounded face and torso, short curved baby arms and legs, glass eyes, black felt nose, brown felt paws, black open mouth, felt tongue, resin claws, and holds a felt fish with glass eyes. Nippy has original brass RJW button, original paper label "R. John Wright, Nippy #65/500", original box with certificate of authenticity and booklet. The model was an exclusive for Campbell's Collectibles, the third in the Baby Bear Collection, and was released in 2000 in a numbered edition of 500. $450/650

88. Joey from the Baby Bear Collection, Exclusive Edition
12". Of grey mohair plush, Joey has rounded face and torso, short
curved baby arms and legs, glass eyes, black resin nose, shaded
muzzle, brown felt paws, resin claws, and holds green felt leaf. Joey
has original brass RJW button, original paper label "R. John Wright,
Joey #65/500", original box with certificate of authenticity and
booklet. The model was released in 2003 as a fund-raiser for Koala
conservation, and was the final edition of the Baby Bear Collection.
$450/650

89. Emma with Crook from Early Character Doll Series
17". Pressed felt character features, broad nose bridge, blue painted
eyes set into deep sockets, thick black upper eyeliner, deep crinkles
around the eyes, brown mohair wig with grey flecks gathered into
bun at nape of neck, swivel head, jointing at shoulders and hips. She
wears a moss-green felt dress, white cutwork apron, petticoat,
pantalets, brown stockings, leather shoes, plaid shawl, black felt
bonnet and carries a wooden crook. The doll has Wright stamp on
its foot, paper label on dress with Vermont address, pencil noted K1-
12. The doll was issued as Emma and was produced from 1979-
1981. $1100/1500

90. Wintertime Christopher Robin, Exclusive Edition

11". Pressed felt face with painted features, brown eyes, downcast pouty mouth, brunette mohair bobbed wig, slender body with jointed limbs. He is wearing green khaki suit under green corduroy raincoat and rain hat, black rubber boots. The doll has original brass RJW button and is contained in original box with wooden sled, and certificate of authenticity labeled #126/250. The doll was released in 1999 in an edition of 250 exclusively for FAO Schwarz. $1000/1400

91. Wintertime Eeyore, Exclusive Edition

5"l. Of taupe mohair, the storybook figure is firmly stuffed, has a blanket of felt "snow" on its back, black mohair mane, black bead eyes, swivel head, jointed legs. He has original brass RJW button and cloth label, and is contained in original box with wooden hut, and certificate of authenticity labeled #5/250. Eeyore was released in 1996 in an edition of 250, exclusively for FAO Schwarz. $600/900

92. Wintertime Pooh and Piglet

5" and 2 3/4". Each is of pressed felt with firmly stuffed body and head, with black bead eyes, Piglet with painted blush, each with jointed limbs. Pooh wears red felt one-button vest and grey scarf; Piglet has green felt costumed body and red felt flyaway scarf. Pooh has brass RJW button and cloth label, and the bear is contained in original deluxe box with colorful illustration, certificate of authenticity labeled #248/250. The pair were released in 1995 in an edition of 500 exclusively for FAO Schwarz. $600/900

93. Pocket Eeyore

6"l. Of taupe mohair, the storybook figure has swivel head, tiny black bead eyes, jointed legs, black mohair mane and tail. He has brass RJW button, cloth label, booklet, and is contained in original box with certificate of authenticity, #3070/3500. $200/300

94. King Christopher Robin, Exclusive Edition

11". Pressed felt swivel head with painted facial features, brunette short bobbed mohair wig, slender body with jointed arms and legs. He is wearing gold paper crown, white jersey shirt, blue shorts, leather belt, long burgundy jacquard cape, leather sandals, white socks, and carrying a toy sword; included is a set of miniature soldiers. He has brass RJW button, paper label "R. John Wright's King Christopher Robin, #9/150" and is contained in original deluxe box with certificate of authenticity. Although the tag indicates an edition of 150, only 50 sets were made. The set was created exclusively for 1998 Expo West doll and teddy bear convention. $1500/2500

96. Musette Candy Container, Exclusive Edition
12". Pressed felt swivel head with unusual facial expression, small blue painted eyes, rounded nose, blonde mohair wig with delicate tendrils around the face and three curled ringlets at back of head, hollow felt torso that separates at waist for use as candy container, jointed felt limbs, wearing maroon silk dress with filled grey/teal felt bodice, organza teal and gold petticoats, pantalets with ruffled edges, felt shoes with burgundy silk bows. She has brass RJW button, paper label "Le Bal Masque, Musette, UFDC New Orleans 2003, R. John Wright", and is in original deluxe gold-edged box with certificate of authenticity. She was released in an edition of 1600 for the 2003 UFDC convention. $500/700

97. Montague Candy Container, Exclusive Edition
12". Pressed felt swivel head with matching facial expression to Musette, brown mohair wig, hollow felt torso that separates at waist for use as a candy container, jointed felt limbs, wearing maroon and teal felt jester costume with fringed and embroidered detail, matching elaborate hat, green felt shoes with maroon silk rosettes, and carrying wooden gold-tipped stick. He has brass RJW button, paper label "Le Bal Masque, Montague, UFDC New Orleans, 2003, R. John Wright" and is in original deluxe gold-edged box with certificate of authenticity. He was released in an edition of 500 for the 2003 UFDC convention. $500/700

98. Klassic Kewpie
8". Pressed felt swivel head with painted side-glancing eyes, tiny nose, thin line smile, topknot with tufts of mohair, blue wings, jointed limbs. Kewpie has brass RJW button and paper label, red heart label, and is in original box with certificate of authenticity indicating #597/1000. Kewpie was released in 1999 in an edition of 1000. $400/600

99. Peppermint Pal Scootles
6 1/2". Pressed felt swivel head with sculpted curly hair, painted facial features, blue side-glancing eyes, beaming smile, jointed arms with trademark thick spread-apart fingers, jointed legs, wearing white felt sun-suit with burgundy felt stripes, matching cap. Scootles has paper label "Kewpie Collection, Peppermint Pal, #24/300 R. John Wright Dolls" that is autographed by the artist, and is in original box with certificate of authenticity. Peppermint Pal was released for the Rose O'Neill luncheon at the UFDC 2003 convention in an edition of 300. $500/700

100. Peppermint Scootles
6 1/2". Pressed felt swivel head with sculpted curly hair, painted facial features, blue side-glancing eyes, beaming smile, jointed arms with trademark thick spread-apart fingers, jointed legs, wearing pink and burgundy striped felt sun-suit, matching pink felt cap with white felt cutwork ruffles. Scootles has paper label "Kewpie Collection, Peppermint, #24/300 R. John Wright Dolls", and is in original box with certificate of authenticity. Peppermint was released for the Rose O'Neill luncheon at the UFDC 2003 convention in an edition of 250. Included is a matching felt napkin ring. $500/700

95. The Enchanted Doll, Exclusive Edition
14". Pressed felt swivel head with painted facial features, unusual bulbous brown eyes, rounded nose, dark brunette long mohair curls, slender arms and legs, wearing pink and white checkered cotton dress with white ruffle, white apron, petticoat, pantalets, matching sunbonnet and parasol, black leather boots. She has brass RJW button, paper label "R. John Wright The Enchanted Doll, Made Exclusively for The Enchanted Doll House, #169/500", and is in original labeled box with letter from the Enchanted Doll House and special cloisonné pin. The doll was released in a numbered edition of 500 in 1989 and featured the yet-unused preliminary Snow White face mold. $700/900

101. Becky from Little Children Series I
17". Pressed felt character head with painted facial features, brown eyes, brunette mohair wig in short braids, jointing at shoulders and hips. Becky is wearing flowered cotton blouse with brown cotton jumper, muslin slip and panties, red leather strap shoes, straw bonnet. She has original gilt/green paper label and another paper label "R. John Wright Becky Little Children Series I, #17/250", and is contained in his original labeled box. The doll was released in 1981-1985 in a numbered edition of 250. $1100/1400

102. Jesse from Little Children Series I
17". Pressed felt character head with painted facial features, brown eyes, brunette side-parted mohair wig, jointing at shoulders and hips. Jesse is wearing khaki cotton jacket with wooden buttons over plaid cotton shirt, green corduroy pants, burgundy felt cap, black stockings, brown leather shoes. He has green/gold paper label and another paper label "R. John Wright Jesse Little Children Series I, #7/250", and is contained in his original labeled box. The model was released in 1981-1985 in a numbered edition of 250. $1000/1400

103. Teddy Roosevelt, Mississippi Bear Hunt

15". Pressed felt character head depicting Teddy Roosevelt, painted facial features includes blue eyes, thick fringed brows, shaded beard, open mouth with painted rows of teeth, with mohair flocked brunette hair and thick moustache, chubby torso, jointed elongated arms and jointed legs, wearing black felt shirt, light grey jacket with belt and pockets, tan felt trousers fitted to his fat belly, grey spats, brown leather shoes, green felt hat, spectacles, ammunition belt with brass bullets, felt appliqué neck scarf, and clasping a little brown alpaca bear cub with jointed limbs and side-glancing eyes, and a wooden and leather rifle that is a replica of the one owned by TR. He has paper label "Teddy Roosevelt Mississippi Bear Hunt, #148/500, R. John Wright Doll" and is in original box with certificate of authenticity. The doll is the first historical portrait doll by R. John Wright Dolls and was released in 2002 in an edition of 500. $1400/1800

104. Millenium Kewpie

8". Pressed felt swivel head with painted side-glancing eyes, tiny nose, thin line smile, topknot, blue wings, jointed limbs, with grey felt chest banner lettered Millenium Kewpie, black top hat and wooden gold-tipped walking stick. Kewpie has brass RJW button and paper label "R. John Wright Millenium Kewpie #71/500", red heart label, and is in original box with certificate of authenticity. He was released in 2000 in an edition of 500. $400/500

105. Bao-Bao, Exclusive Edition

12". Of white and black firmly stuffed mohair, the baby panda bear has black masks around the glass eyes, open mouth with black felt lining and shaded pink tongue, resin nose, jointed arms and legs, resin claws, brown felt paws, and is holding a green leaf. He has brass RJW button on back and paper label "R. John Wright Baby Bear Collection, Bao-Bao, Made for Precious Things, #93/500". The bear is in its original deluxe box with illustration, booklet and certificate of authenticity. It was an exclusive edition for Precious Things of Singapore. $400/500

106. Pooh-Bee, Exclusive Edition

8". Light brown mohair Pooh teddy has brown embroidered nose, small black bead eyes, chubby torso, and short plump limbs with bent right arm. Pooh is wearing a removable bumble-bee costume of yellow and black striped felt with black fitted cap having stinger, and clasping a felt flowered clover. He has brass RJW button, and paper

label "Winnie the Pooh, Pooh Bee, Made for Teddys, #281/500, R. John Wright" and is in original labeled box with certificate of authenticity. The bear was made exclusively for the teddy bear shop, Teddys in 1999 in a numbered edition of 500. $400/600

107. Kewpie Chick

7". Pressed felt swivel head with painted side-glancing eyes, tiny nose, thin line smile, jointed felt arms, brown felt jointed chicken legs, wearing yellow mohair chicken suit (removable) with fitted hood, brown felt tip, felt-lined yellow wings. Kewpie Chick has brass RJW button and paper label "R. John Wright Kewpie Chick #245/250" and is in original box with certificate of authenticity. He was released in 2002 in a numbered edition of 250. $400/500

108. Maria with Orange Cummerbund from Early Character Doll Series

17". Pressed felt character features, pointy nose, brown side-glancing painted eyes, smiling expression, black mohair wig in long braid, swivel head, jointing at shoulders and hips. She wears a long dress with pale green top over white blouse, flowered skirt, orange felt laced cummerbund with matching felt shoes, petticoat, and panties. The doll has Wright stamp on its foot and paper label with Vermont address. The doll was issued as Maria and was produced from 1977-1978. $1100/1500

109. Mario with Burgundy Vest from Early Character Doll Series

17". Pressed felt character features, broad nose bridge, brown painted eyes in deeply set eye sockets, deep crinkles under eyes, very thick bushy mohair moustache, black mohair tousled hair, swivel head, jointing at shoulders and hips. He wears a white cotton pin-dotted shirt, burgundy felt vest, brown felt cap, plaid cotton pants, and black leather shoes. The doll has Wright stamp on its foot. The doll was issued as Mario and was produced from 1977-1978. $1100/1500

110. Maria with Brown Cummerbund from Early Character Doll Series

17". Pressed felt character features, pointy nose, brown side-glancing painted eyes, smiling expression, black mohair wig in long braid, swivel head, jointing at shoulders and hips. She wears a long dress with lavender top over white dotted Swiss blouse,, flowered skirt, brown felt laced cummerbund with matching felt shoes, petticoat, and panties. The doll has Wright stamp on its foot and paper label with Vermont address and hand-lettered "Maria". The doll was issued as Maria and was produced from 1977-1978. $1100/1500

111. Elizabeth from Little Children, Series I

17". Pressed felt character head with painted facial features, blue eyes, brunette mohair wig, jointing at shoulders and hips. Elizabeth is wearing dusty-rose cotton dress, white pinafore, muslin slip and panties, socks, black leather strap shoes. She has R. John Wright stamp on foot, original gilt/green paper label and another paper label "R. John Wright Elizabeth Little Children Series I, #17/250", and is contained in her original labeled box. The doll was released in 1981-1985 in a numbered edition of 250. $1000/1300

112. Maria with Brown Cummerbund from Early Character Doll Series

17". Pressed felt character features, pointy nose, brown side-glancing painted eyes, smiling expression, brown mohair wig in long braid, swivel head, jointing at shoulders and hips. She wears a long dress with blue top over white blouse, flowered skirt, brown felt laced cummerbund with matching felt shoes, petticoat, and panties. The doll has Wright stamp on its foot. The doll was issued as Maria and was produced from 1977-1978. $1100/1500

113. Classic Winnie the Pooh with Pin

13". Of light brown mohair, with rounded head and protruding snout, chubby torso, jointed curved arms, hip-jointed short legs, glass eyes, brown embroidered nose, wearing red stockinette one-button vest and large celluloid button with photograph of the bear. With brass RJW button and paper label "R. John Wright Classic Winnie the Pooh, #267/2500", and in gold-lettered felt sack with drawstring top and certificate of authenticity. Pooh was released in 1998 in a numbered edition of 2500. $400/600

114. Silly Old Bear

7". Of brown shaved mohair plush, with double face seam on angular head, small ears, black bead eyes, swivel head, pellet-stuffed body, jointed arms and legs, with brass RJW button paper label "Silly Old Bear, #473", in green drawstring sack with certificate of authenticity. The piece was released as an exclusive Collector's Club edition in 1998-1999 and 720 pieces were produced. $400/500

115. Black Bitty Bear
3 1/2". Black mohair teddy has swivel head, jointed limbs, black bead eyesyellow felt ruffled collar, brass RJW button, and green felt pouch with certificate of authenticity indicating #253/350. The bear was released in 2003 in an edition of 350. $200/300

116. Boutonniere Kewpie
2". Pressed felt Kewpie is posed with outstretched arms, legs together, painted side-glancing eyes, painted wings, red heart label, brass clip on reverse for use as boutonniere. Kewpie has a tag under the clasp indicating #241. Kewpie is in original box with certificate of authenticity and was released in 2001 in an edition of 1000. $200/300

117. Jemima Puddle Duck
15". Fluffy white mohair duck with s-curved neck, swivel head, glass eyes, yellow felt beak and feet, movable wings, wearing fringed shawl and blue sunbonnet, with brass RJW button and paper label "Jemima Puddle-Duck, R. John Wright, #281/1500" and in original deluxe box with color illustration on lid and certificate of authenticity. Jemima Puddle-Duck, from the Beatrix Potter Collection, was released in 2000 in an edition of 1500. $500/700

118. Mrs Rabbitt
15". White mohair plush with delicately shaded brown color, pink felt lined ears with shaded color, large glass eyes, swivel head, jointed limbs, wearing blue cotton dress, shawl, white apron, striped felt petticoat, leather buckle shoes, with original paper label "Mrs Rabbit #281/500, R. John Wright" and brass RJW button, and in original deluxe labeled box with certificate of authenticity. Mrs. Rabbit, from the Beatrix Potter Collection was released in 2004 in an edition of 500. $500/700

119. Peter Rabbit
8". Fluffy white mohair with delicately shaded brown highlights, shaded pink felt lined ears, glass eyes, whiskers, swivel head, jointed short curved arms, unusual jointed legs with very wide hips and tiny feet, blue felt jacket with brass buttons, leather slippers. Original paper label "Beatrix Potter Collection, Peter, #279/500, R. John Wright" and original box with certificate of authenticity. Peter was released in 2003. $400/600

120. Benjamin Bunny
12". Fluffy white mohair with shaded brown coloring especially of upper face, large black glass eyes on brown felt circles, pink felt lined ears, jointed arms and legs with very wide hips and tiny feet, wearing brown felt jacket with marble-colored buttons, green knit over-sized cap with orange pom-pom, orange cotton scarf, leather clogs with buckles and carrying a felt and organdy onion. With brass RJW button, paper label "Beatrix Potter Collection, Benjamin Bunny, #281/1500 R. John Wright" and original box with story booklet and certificate of authenticity. Benjamin was released in 2001 in a numbered edition. $500/700

121. Flopsy, Mopsy and Cottontail
Each 8". Each of fluffy white mohair with shaded brown coloring, shaded pink felt lined ears, whiskers, glass eyes, swivel head, jointed limbs, wearing orange velvet lined cape and carrying wicker basket with felt fruit and vegetables. Each has brass RJW button and paper label with name of bunny (Flopsy, Mopsy or Cottontail) and "#125/500", in original deluxe box with colorful illustration on lid, story booklet and certificate of authenticity on inside. The set was issued in 2003 in a numbered edition of 500. $800/1000

122. Peter Rabbit without Whiskers

8". Fluffy white mohair with delicately shaded brown highlights, brown felt lined ears, glass eyes, swivel head, jointed short curved arms, unusual jointed legs with very wide hips and tiny feet, blue felt jacket with brass buttons, leather slippers, carrying felt English radish with green stems. Original paper label "Beatrix Potter Collection, Peter, #524/2500, R. John Wright" and original box with certificate of authenticity. Peter was released in 1998. $500/700

123. The Flopsy Bunnies

Each 5 1/2". Six baby bunnies are posed as though sleeping around a large cabbage, each bunny of shaded brown white mohair, lying on back with curled limbs, head tucked into tummy, stitched closed eyes, pink felt lined ears, each with brass RJW button. The cabbage of stiffened, painted green felt is posed upon a felt-covered earth-like base. With original paper label "420/500" on cabbage, and storybook and certificate of authenticity in deluxe box with color illustration. The set was issued in 2001 in a numbered edition of 500. $900/1100

124. Peter Rabbit with Whiskers
8". Fluffy white mohair with delicately shaded brown highlights, brown felt lined ears, glass eyes, long whiskers, swivel head, jointed short curved arms, unusual jointed legs with very wide hips and tiny feet, blue felt jacket with brass buttons, leather slippers, carrying felt English radish with green stems. Original paper label "Beatrix Potter Collection, Peter, #1548/2500, R. John Wright" and original box with certificate of authenticity. Peter was released in 1998. $400/600

125. Beatrix Potter Garden Wheelbarrow
12"l. Weathered yellow pine wooden wheelbarrow with jointed wheel is filled with felt vegetables including cabbage, carrot, turnip, onions, and such, each with shaded coloring of leaves, each with brass RJW button. With original paper label "Beatrix Potter Collection, Garden Wheelbarrow, #281/500, R. John Wright", and in original box with certificate of authenticity. The wheelbarrow was released in 2001 in a numbered edition of 500. $300/500

126. Kewpie Bunny
6". Pressed felt doll with painted facial features, side-glancing eyes, swivel head, blue wings, jointed limbs, wearing removable white felt bunny suit with pink buttons, fitted hood with pink-lined bunny hears, with wicker basket and Easter eggs, with brass RJW button and paper label "R. John Wright, Kewpie Bunny, #202/250", and in original box with certificate of authenticity. $300/400

127. Tom Kitten
11". Of white mohair plush with prominent brown tabby coloring, pink felt lined ears, green glass eyes, freckles with whiskers, jointed arms and legs, metal self stand, blue cotton romper suit and straw hat, brass RJW button, original paper label "Beatrix Potter Collection, Tom Kitten #346/1500", with original box and certificate of authenticity. Tom was released in 2003 in a numbered edition of 1500. $400/600

128. Mittens
11". Of white mohair with very prominent shaded brown tabby coloring, freckles with whisklers, felt lined ears, green glass eyes, pink nose, jointed arms and legs, wearing white cotton pinafore dress, metal self stand, with brass RJW button and paper label "Beatrix Potter Collection Mittens, #281/500", with original box and certificate of authenticity. Mittens was released in 2004 in a numbered edition of 500. $400/600

Other Doll Artists

Exceptional works by American and European doll artists are shown in this section. Some are virtual unknowns, their apparent talents and artistry having not been matched by their marketing ability, or their artistic life cut short by illness or death. Many of the artists are well-known, their dolls having won awards and already earned the support of keen-eyed collectors. There is this paradox of the doll artist world that recognition of quality breeds demand. Artists have sought to meet that demand in various ways, some staying true to only creating one-of-a-kind dolls, others creating very limited editions and sometimes enlisting the aid of talented artists or family in the creation of costumes or wig-making, and still others who seek to please the clamoring public by designing dolls for commercial production, while still continuing to design and make unique dolls bearing their personal signature.

Jane Davies, English doll artist, is noted for her porcelain miniature and dollhouse dolls. A member of NIADA, she is adamant that each aspect of her doll work must be her own, from conception, to painting, to costuming.

129. Pair, Boy and Girl in Knit Costumes by Jane Davies
Each 5". Each is all-bisque with shaded brown complexion, realistically sculpted features (she smiling, he pouty), she with black wig, he with painted hair, each with jointing at shoulders, hips, elbows and wrists, wearing knit middy costumes, white socks and sandals. Each signed "JD 1996". $300/400

130. Washie in Blue Suit with Bunny by Jane Davies
5". All-bisque boy with swivel head and waist, jointing at shoulders, hips and elbows, painted facial features, painted shoes, blonde hair, blue cotton suit in the 18th century style, holding articulated velvet bunny. Signed "JSD 1988 Washie". $200/300

131. Nellie in Peach Gown with Hoops by Jane Davies
5". All-bisque girl with swivel head and waist, jointing at shoulders, hips, elbows and wrists, painted facial features, painted shoes, auburn hair, pale peach gown, holding flower decorated hoops. Signed "JSD 1988 Nellie". $200/300

132. William in Sailor Suit by Jane Davies

4 1/2". All-bisque boy with swivel head, jointing at shoulders, hips, elbows and wrists, painted facial features, painted shoes, auburn short hair, wearing sailor suit with straw hat. Signed "JSD 1988 William". $200/300

133. Zara in Party Dress by Jane Davies

5". All-bisque girl with swivel head and waist, jointing at shoulders and hips, painted facial features, painted ribbed stockings and peach party shoes with sculpted bows, wearing peach silk party dress with lace trim. Signed "JSD 1988 Zara". $200/300

134. Bisque Character Girl with Teddy by Wiltrud Stein

15". Bisque head with rounded shoulder plate, enamel painted eyes in sculpted sockets, beautifully painted features, pouty expression, wispy hand-knotted mohair wig with braids, soft cloth body, bisque hands with curled fingers, bisque legs to above the knees, wearing a cotton print dress, woolen knit pants and socks, brown leather shoes with straps, and holding a little mohair teddy with muslin and lace dress. The doll is signed "Wiltrud 90 A 2/10" and has wrist tag "Wiltrud". The pouty girl was made by German artist Wiltrud Stein in 1990, in a numbered edition of ten dolls. The German artist began her career in 1983 and was won many awards for her artistic creations. Each of her dolls is sculpted, hand-painted and costumed completely by the artist. $500/700

Regina Sandreuter, the German-born artist who has studied and worked in Germany, India, France and Switzerland has been inspired by the early 20th century art character dolls, the highly expressive faces of the bisque movement, and the infinite articulation and durability of the wooden-bodied Schoenhut doll. Her early art dolls, made entirely of finely grained wood, artfully carved, tinted and naturally finished, were constructed at first with an eight-part body, and shortly thereafter with a trademarked 12-part Multi-pose body designed by the artist and her collaborator husband. Because of the intensive hand-workmanship, the dolls have always been of very limited editions.

135. Fiona by Regina Sandreuter

17 1/2". All wooden doll with swivel head, carved facial features enhanced to capture the grain of the wood in an artistic manner, painted brown eyes with black and grey upper eyeliner, painted lashes, fringed brows, closed mouth with pouty expression, hand-tied mohair wig, trademark 12-part Multipose body with hidden joints, wearing artist-made flowered cotton dress, homespun-like apron with pocket and button to match dress, one piece undergarment, stockings, kidskin shoes. The doll is signed "1991 F6 31" on the head and has wrist tag with name "Fiona". The doll was made in 1991, #31 in a numbered edition of 75.
$1800/2500

136. Monika by Regina Sandreuter

17". All-wooden doll with swivel head, slender face and elongated throat, painted shaded blue eyes, fringed lashes and brows, rounded broad nose, shaded lips, golden auburn mohair wig with wispy curls, trademark 12-part Multipose body with swivel waist and elbows, jointing at shoulders, elbows, hips and knees designed to be hidden when doll is standing upright, wearing cotton print one piece romper suit, red leather sandals. The doll is signed "RSI Sandreuter 1993 M68 girl" on the head and "Monika c. 1993" inside the costume. She has original paper wrist label, and is #68 from an edition of 150 dolls. The doll was made in 1993. $1800/2200

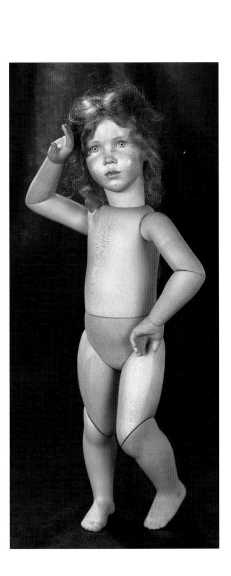

137. Red-haired Boy by Regina Sandreuter

17". All-wooden doll with swivel head, slender face with intelligent expression, elongated throat, darker complexion, painted shaded green eyes with fringed brows and lashes, blushed cheeks, brunette-reddish mohair wig, eight-part wooden body with swivel waist, jointing at shoulders, hips and knees, wearing brown cotton shirt with smocking detail, corduroy pants with suspenders, stockings, ankle boots. The doll is marked "RSI Sandreuter" on her head and has a tag in costume "JT 8 1988". The doll was made in 1988. $1200/1600

138. Girl with Long Brunette Curls by Regina Sandreuter

17". All wooden doll with swivel head, glowing complexion, outlined painted blue eyes, fringed brows and lashes, rounded nose, blushed cheeks, brunette hair in wispy side curls with pony tail at back, eight-part wooden body with swivel waist, jointing at shoulders, hips and knees, wearing linen-like jacket with sienna cotton trim and underblouse, wonderfully patterned harem-style pants, rust suede ankle shoes. The doll is marked "RSI Sandreuter 1993" on her head and has a tag in costume "GI 42 c.1993. 42/45" and has original wrist tag. The doll was made in 1993 in an edition of 45. $1200/1600

139. Brown-Eyed Girl by Regina Sandreuter

17". All wooden doll with swivel head, painted brown eyes with fringed lashes and brows, nicely blushed cheeks and chin, brunette mohair wig with wispy side curls and braid at back, eight-part wooden body with swivel waist, jointing at shoulders, hips and knees, wearing red cotton lapel blouse with textured vest, patterned harem-style pants, brown kidskin ankle boots. The doll is marked "RSI Sandreuter 1989" on her head, and has a label in costume "DW 16 c.1989". The doll was made in 1989. $1200/1600

140. Brunette Haired Girl in Striped Dress, ST 14, by Regina Sandreuter

18". All wooden doll with swivel head, carved facial features with elongated throat, upper glancing painted blue eyes, upturned nose, fringed lashes and brows, closed mouth, brunette mohair wig, eight-piece body with swivel waist, jointing at shoulders, hips and knees, carved bent elbows, wearing cotton dress with blue and green striped skirt and sleeves, one piece undergarments, shoes and socks. The doll is signed "RS Sandreuter" on the head and dress tag hand-lettered "ST 14 1988". The doll was made in 1988. $1200/1500

141. Brown-eyed Boy with 12-Part Body by Regina Sandreuter

18". All wooden doll with swivel head, carved facial features, painted lashes and brows, shaded brown eyes, closed mouth, details of carving include dimples and philtrum, softly blushed complexion, brunette mohair wig, 12 part Multi-pose body with swivel waist and wrists, jointing at shoulders, elbows, hips and knees, wearing plaid brown and red shirt with twill faded red pants, leather straps, shoes and shoes. The doll is signed "Sandreuter RSI c.1993 M44 Boy" and has original paper wrist tag noting that that the doll is #44 from an edition of 50. The doll was made in 1993. $1800/2500

142. Blue-Eyed Felix by Regina Sandreuter

18". All-wooden doll with swivel head, very full chubby cheeks, blue eyes, upturned nose, blushed cheeks, blonde mohair bobbed wig, 12-part Multi-pose body with swivel waist and wrists, jointing at shoulders, elbows, hips and knees with hidden joints, wearing knit sweater and wonderfully patterned woven suspender pants with floral waistband and cuffs, grey kidskin shoes. The doll is signed "RSI Sandreuter 1991 F57 Boy" on head, and the costume is tagged "Felix 1990 57. The doll was made in 1991 in an edition of 75 of which this is #57. $1800/2500

143. Samantha by Patricia Wall

20". Bisque head on bisque shoulder plate with rich brown complexion, eyes painted as though sleeping, slightly open mouth with tongue tip, blushed cheeks, black mohair wig with cloth ribbons, cloth body, bisque lower arms and legs, wearing red checkered cotton dress under pinafore, undergarments, black stockings, leather shoes, and holding wooden knitting needles and half-finished scarf, posed seated on green wooden ladder back chair with pot belly stove and basket of yarn. The doll is signed "1989 Patricia Wall 13/30", and has original certificate of authenticity. Included is a November 1989 note from the artist with a colorful print of the original early 20th century lithograph "Woman's Work is Never Done" which inspired the doll. The doll was made in 1989 in an edition of 30. $800/1100

Munich artist Elisabeth Pongratz has created a series of dolls in the tradition of early 20th century doll artist Marion Kaulitz, although her choice of medium (wood) differs from that earlier artist. Fittingly her dolls are known as "New Munich Art Dolls". They are notable for a seeming simplicity of carving and painting, yet are utterly captivating in their innocence and artfulness of expression. The grain of the wood is positioned to enhance the carving, and delicately tinted for a nuanced complexion. Her dolls are entirely designed, created and dressed by herself, and are made in extremely limited edition, usually of less than 10.

144. Black-Complexioned New Munich Art Doll by Elisabeth Pongratz

14". All wooden doll with socket head, lightly tinted and softly blushed conplexion with painted brown eyes, closed mouth with pouty expression, very soft mohair fleecy hair, all wooden body with shoulder and hip spring-jointing, carved mitten hands with separate thumb, wearing blue hand-knit dress, black knit socks, black suede shoes. The doll has original hang tag with artist's name and address, and is hand-lettered "H12ON". $1100/1300

145. Blonde-Haired Girl New Munich Art Doll by Elisabeth Pongratz

14". Carved wooden socket head with lightly blushed complexion, small painted blue eyes delicately tinted pouty lips, very soft blonde mohair wig in braids, unusual peach muslin body with disc-jointing at shoulders and hips. The doll in unmarked. $800/1200

146. Painted Hair New Munich Art Doll by Elizabeth Pongratz

14". Carved wooden socket head, painted short brown hair with stippling detail, painted blue eyes with large black pupils, delicately tinted pouty lips, all wooden body with spring jointing at shoulders and hips, carved mitten hands with separate thumbs, wearing original knit dress with scalloped edging, three-button yoke, matching cap and socks, red suede ankle shoes, white cotton knitted undergarment, and with original wooden stand, marked on foot "83B1514P". The doll was made in 1983 and is an unusual model with painted hair. $1100/1500

147. Zudie's Coverlet by Wendy Lawton with Wooden Articulated Body

16". Brown-complexioned bisque doll, brown glass eyes, closed mouth with painted teeth, black tightly curled hair with narrow braids, wooden carved body with jointing at shoulders, elbows, wrists, hips, knees and ankles, bisque hands, wearing calico print cotton dress with diamond-patterned borders and large hair bow, and owning a beautiful miniature quilt with folk-art hand-dyed designs along with wooden frame for display. The doll also owns woolen pleated skirt, burgundy corduroy skirt, two hand-knitted vests, and Irish knit cardigan The doll is marked 79/350 Lawton 1996, and has hang tag and certificate of authenticity "Fabrics of America Series, Zudie's Coverlet...". Dress and quilt have Wendy Lawton cloth labels. Original box included. $800/1100

Ther Nuremberg, Germany Artist Almut Augustin created dolls during the 1980's until her death in 1992. The doll costumes were made by her sister.

148. Girl in Red Sweater
by Almut Augustin

13". Carved wooden head with flanged neck and very characterized face, painted facial features, shaded blue eyes, brunette mohair wig, cloth torso and hip-jointed legs, wooden arms to above the elbows, carved cupped hands, wearing original blouse, blue woolen pinafore, red knit sweater, stockings, shoes, yellow leather school bag and having original wooden hang tag "Original Almut Augustin". The doll was made in the late 1980's. $400/500

149. Toddler in Lavender Overalls
by Almut Augustin

12". Carved wooden head with flanged neck, expressive toddler features with wide cheeks, painted shaded brown eyes, long brunette hair, cloth body with jointing at shoulders and hips, carved wooden hands with left hand positioned to hold an object, wearing pink cotton blouse, lavender patterned overalls, white shoes, white knit cap, with original wooden hang tag "Original Almut Augustin" and signed "AA 1986" on the head. The doll was made in 1986. $400/500

150. Wooden Doll by Karin Schmitt

15". Carved wooden head with painted facial features, large brown eyes, pouty expression, brunette curly hair, cloth body with wooden legs to above the knees, and wooden arms to just below elbows, separately carved fingers. Wearing brown checkered cotton dress, apron, undergarments, carrying document naming the doll "Katia". The doll is signed on back of head "1990 K. Schmidt" with paper label "Structura". $300/400

151. Bisque Girl with Young Baby by Sylvia Natterer

21". Bisque swivel-head on bisque shoulder plate with golden-sienna tinted complexion depicts an older girl, having painted facial features, brown eyes, full lips, black human hair in delicate braids, cloth body with bisque lower arms and legs, bare feet. The girl is carrying a bisque-head baby with painted features. Each doll wears original artist-made costume of with superb detail of fabrics and construction, and the girl carries a spool of flax for weaving and a hand-woven carpet. The doll is marked "Sylvia Natterer 1989 NS 5". The doll was handmade and costumed by the artist in 1989, and is a stunningly beautiful work of art. $2000/2500

152. Porcelain Young Girl by Robert Tonner

18". Bisque head with superbly sculpted and painted facial features depicting a young girl, very characterized and intelligent features and expression, light brown curly mohair wig, cloth body with bisque sculpted hands and legs to mid-thing, wearing artist made navy knit long sweater, white collar, pleated plaid skirt and bow, blue woolen beret, white tights and sturdy-appearing brown school shoes. The doll is marked "Robert Tonner" and was made by the artist about 1990 in a total series of ten dolls, each costumed uniquely. $1200/1600

153. Kidskin Doll by Beate Schult

14". Very soft kidskin leather doll with separately stitched face onto leather head dome, whitened complexion with artfully painted facial features, brown eyes, eye shadow, shaded lips, white mohair fleeced wig, intricately stitched all-leather body with tri-color leather, wearing original homespun smock with laced shoulders, signed "BS

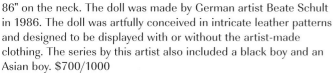

86" on the neck. The doll was made by German artist Beate Schult in 1986. The doll was artfully conceived in intricate leather patterns and designed to be displayed with or without the artist-made clothing. The series by this artist also included a black boy and an Asian boy. $700/1000

154. Kidskin Doll by Maloy Aneelin
14". Pressed and oil painted leather face and lower limbs, inset enamel eyes, upturned nose, artistically painted features, blonde mohair wig, soft cloth body, defined fingers and toes, wearing artist made white pinafore, undergarments, shoes and socks, knit cap. The doll is signed on her left foot "Maloy Anneelin 1995 20/50". $400/500

155. Cloth Doll by Christine Adams
15". All cloth doll with hard-pressed and oil painted face, painted facial features, blue eyes, closed mouth with accented lips, plump cheeks, brunette mohair wig, softly stuffed body with disc-jointed legs, stitch-jointed shoulders, wearing artist-made cotton dress with knit collar, red heavy knit stockings, white kidskin shoes, red knit cap, slip, knit undergarment. The doll is signed "CA Adams 011", and has an original tag "Christine Adams HandMade Dolls, Tiny Tots" that is hand-signed CA Adams 1982. $500/700

156. Gretta by Maggie Iacono

15". All felt doll, swivel head with press-sculpted facial features, shadowed complexion, painted brown eyes, long blonde mohair braids, felt body jointed at shoulder and hips, wearing artist made brown felt vest over white shirt, brown skirt with flowered apron, checkered petticoat, pantalets, stockings, brown leather shoes, scarf. The doll has original paper label "Maggie Made Dolls and Bears, Gretta, 27/250", and original certificate of authenticity indicating 1991 year of production edition limited to 250 dolls. $700/1000

157. Shelby by Maggie Iacono

15". All felt doll, swivel head with smooth-finish felt sculpted face, painted facial features, brown shaded eyes, closed mouth, long blonde human hair, articulated 11-piece felt body with wooden ball-jointing at shoulders, elbows, hips, and knees that allows the doll to hold its pose, swivel ankles, wearing white cotton lattice-patterned dress with long eyelet cut petticoat and pantalets, shoes, sash, straw bonnet with flowers. The doll has original paper label "Maggie-Made Shelby 18/75", and is hand-signed "Iacono c. 93" on left foot. The shoes are also signed, and the doll has a certificate of authenticity, and original box with gold paper label. The doll was made in 1993 in an edition of 75 dolls. $800/1200

The American artist, Maggie Iacono, describes her dolls as "expressions in felt", and when asked her profession she says simply "I'm an artist". Asked to explain, she adds that she is an artist whose métier is the doll. She creates all aspects of her dolls, from their hand-painted faces to their handmade dolls, so, in essence, each doll is unique even though made in small editions. The artist is an elected member of NIADA and has received many awards for her dolls.

158. Alexandra by Maggie Iacono

15". All felt doll, swivel head with smooth-finish felt sculpted face, painted facial features, brown shaded eyes, closed mouth, long red mohair wig, brown painted eyes, closed mouth, armature-framed felt body jointed at shoulder and hips, wearing blue woolen pleated skirt, burgundy felt middy jacket and matching hat, undergarments, leggings, black leather shoes. The doll has original paper label "Maggie Made Alexandra 26/150" and original certificate of authenticity, and original box with gold paper label. The doll was made in 1991 in an edition of 150 dolls. $800/1200

159. Corey by Maggie Iacono

15". All felt doll, swivel head with smooth-finish felt sculpted face, painted facial features, brown shaded eyes, closed mouth, long brunette human hair, articulated 11-piece felt body with wooden ball-jointing at shoulders, elbows, hips, and knees that allows the doll to hold its pose, wearing white cotton dress under grey woolen capelet coat, red wooden beret with matching signed shoes, swivel ankles, white knit socks, petticoat and pantalets. The doll has original paper label "Maggie-Made Corey 17/75", and is hand-signed "Iacono c. 95" on left foot. The shoes are also signed, and the doll has a certificate of authenticity, and original box with gold paper label. The doll was made in 1995 in an edition of 75 dolls. $800/1200

160. Alice by Maggie Iacono

15". All felt doll, swivel head with smooth-finish felt sculpted face, painted facial features, blue shaded eyes, closed mouth, dark blonde human hair, articulated 11-piece felt body with wooden ball-jointing at shoulders, elbows, hips, and knees that allows the doll to hold its pose, swivel ankles, wearing blue felt dress with hand-painted designs, white apron with two pockets, white knit socks, black felt shoes, and pantalets. The doll has original paper label "Maggie-Made Dolls Corey 11/150", and is hand-signed "M. Iacono". The shoes are also signed, and the doll has a certificate of authenticity, and original box with colorful illustration. The doll was made in 1996 in an edition of 150 dolls. $800/1200

161. Goldie Bear by Maggie Iacono

9". Golden mohair teddy with pressed felt muzzle, brown glass eyes, embroidered nose and mouth, jointed limbs, swivel head, felt paw pads, wearing green felt dress with white sleeves and collar, felt appliqué flowers, with cloth label on bear and certificate of authenticity indicating "Maggie Made, 17/250" and 1996 year of production and signed by the artist. The doll is included in its original box. $200/300

162. Elise by Maggie Iacono

17". All felt doll, swivel head with smooth-finish felt sculpted face, painted facial features, brown shaded eyes, closed mouth, dark blonde human hair with ringlet curls and braided coronet, articulated 11-piece felt body with wooden ball-jointing at shoulders, elbows, hips, and knees that allows the doll to hold its pose, swivel ankles, wearing blue and green felt dress with hand-painted bunny designs, white flannel blouse, white knit socks, black felt shoes, petticoat and pantalets. The doll has original paper label "Maggie-Made Dolls Elise 37/75", and is hand-signed "M. Iacono '96". The shoes are also signed, and the doll has a certificate of authenticity, and original box with colorful illustration. The doll was made in 1996 in an edition of 75 dolls. $800/1200

163. Gwyneth by Maggie Iacono

18". All felt doll depicting young lady with slender elongated shape, swivel head with heart-shaped face, painted blue eyes, very full lips, blonde human hair wig drawn into braid at the back of head with wispy curls around the face, female shape to the torso, ball-jointing at shoulders, elbows, hips and knees, and swivel ankles, wearing white sheer cotton summer dress with hand-painted designs, embroidered shawl, sash, petticoat, pants, leather sandals, green beaded necklace, felt broad-brimmed hat with felt appliqué violets and curled stems. The doll has original paper label "Maggie-Made Dolls Gwyneth 25/70", and is hand-signed "M.Iacono '02" on her back. The shoes are also signed and the doll has a certificate of authenticity and original box with colorful illustrations. The doll was made in 2002 in an edition of 70 dolls. $1000/1300

The American artist, Helen Kish, has been sculpting dolls since 1979. A member of NIADA since 1981 she served as its president in 1991. Her African Madonna, which she has described as having the flavor of Africa, rather than expressing a particular tribe, was designed by the artist to "express the universality of the mother/child bond and the regal dignity of the woman". The doll was featured in a full page photograph in the 1992 book, The Art of the Doll, published by NIADA.

164. The African Madonna with Two Children by Helen Kish

21". Portrait doll of slender adult woman, made entirely of bisque and sewn leather, fine sienna brown complexion, featuring an adult woman with slender face, elongated throat, artistically painted facial features, swivel waist, jointed shoulders, needle-sculpted leather lower torso and upper legs, wearing rich costume of colorful fabrics, and posed upon a leather covered stand. Standing alongside her is an 11" child with fleeced hair, painted features, jointed arms and legs, bare feet, and she holds a 4" all bisque baby with jointed arms, and bent baby legs. Each piece is signed by the artist, Helen Kish, and numbered 12/25, 1989. The set was created by the American artist in 1989 in a numbered edition of 25. $1800/2500

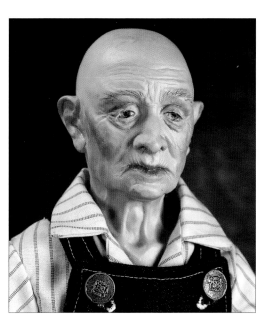

165. The Old Man by Susan Dunham

21". Portrait doll depicting an aged man, bisque head and upper torso, bald pate, very wrinkled facial visage with excellent definition of ears, throat, painted facial features, deeply inset painted eyes, padded cloth armature body, shirt and overall jeans, marked #12 on doll, and with original paper label "World class artist dolls by Susan Dunham" and ink noted "1984 The Old Man, 12/24, Susan Dunham". The doll was created in 1984 by the American artist in an edition of 24. $500/700

Nancy Walters, American artist, describes her works as "people dolls". No molds are created for her dolls; each is one-of-a-kind, with expressively sculpted and hand-painted facial features and hands.

166. Grace, One-of-a-Kind Doll by Nancy Walters

13" seated. Portrait doll depicting an aged woman, bisque shoulder head with very characterized features, sculpted wrinkles, strong nose, inset painted eyes with mauve eye shadow, grey eyebrows, white mohair wig, bisque hands and legs in bent position with fine definition of sculpted toes and fingers. The doll is posed seated, wearing artist made costume, and is signed c.1989 Nancy Walters, and has paper label hand-lettered "Grace, a one-of-a-kind porcelain doll, Nancy Walters". $400/600

167. Wooden Doll with Carved Hair and Bow

13". All wooden doll has carved socket head, painted facial features, elaborately carved hair with curls around the face, ringlet curled ponytail sculpted away from head and decorated by sculpted bow, all-wooden spring-jointed body, wearing white cotton dress with smocking, undergarments, leather shoes. The doll is unmarked. $300/400

The English doll artist pair of Lynne and Michael Roche have been making original design dolls for 25 years, beginning in 1980. Their dolls are made of porcelain, wood or cloth or various combinations, and are notable for intricate articulation, delicate quality of bisque and painting, and fine quality of enamel eyes and soft real hair wigs.

168. Beth by Lynne and Michael Roche
18". Having bisque head with brown glass eyes, reddish brown human hair with bangs, all-wooden ball-jointed body, bisque swivel-jointed hands, wearing blue jersey shirt, blue denim overalls with colorful buttons and ruffle and "Mussels" applique, white socks, red shoes, signed on head "1989 Lynne & Michael Roche" and "Medium Beth 28". The doll was made in 1989 in a limited edition of which this is #28. $900/1200

169. Anna by Lynne and Michael Roche
20". Having bisque head with distinctive portrait like expression, brown eyes, reddish brown human hair, pierced ears, all-wooden ball-jointed body, bisque swivel-jointed hands, wearing knit moss green sweater with russet border, pearl buttons that match the earrings, silk headband, green silk skirt, undergarments, black leggings, black sandals, signed "Anna auburn 16/100 Lynn & Michael Roche" and with original paper tag signed by the artist and dated 1992. The doll, designed to be sold with doll #171, Polly, were presented as Mother and Child; they are both #16 from the edition of 100 made in 1992. $900/1200

170. Lizzie with Punch and Judy by Lynne and Michael Roche
14". Having bisque head with blue glass eyes, brunette human hair pigtails, all-wooden ball-jointed body, bisque swivel-jointed hands, wearing knit playsuit comprising sienna jump suit, golden tunic with sienna and blue ruffles and edging, leather shoes, and owning four miniature hand-knit hand puppets. The doll is marked "Lizzie with Punch and Judy, Special Edition for Toy Shoppe 6/30, 1995" and has original paper label signed by the artists Lynne & Michael Roche. $900/1200

171. Polly by Lynne and Michael Roche
14". Having bisque head with brown glass eyes, brunette human hair, soft-pellet-filled cloth body designed to be held by mother (#169), wearing golden knit sweater and cotton print jumper, with enamel teddy bear pin, and brown felt teddy bear neck purse, socks, white leather shoes, signed "Polly model child, 16/100" and with original artist-signed paper label. The doll was made in 1992, #16 from an edition of 100, and designed as a partner doll to her mother (#169 above). $400/500

172. Katy by Lynne and Michael Roche

18". Having bisque head with brown glass eyes, reddish blonde human hair, all-wooden ball-jointed body, bisque swivel hands, wearing plaid red and cream romper suit with matching skirt, cream jacket with plaid edging and embroidery, stockings, shoes, signed "Katy Off To the Beach, specially for The Toy Shoppe 2/10 c. 1994 Lynne & Michael Roche", and with original paper wrist tag signed by the artists. The doll was made in 1994, an exclusive limited edition of 10. $900/1200

173. Colette by Lynne and Michael Roche

17". Having plump bisque head with blue glass eyes, blonde human hair wig, all-wooden ball-jointed body with plump shaping, bisque swivel hands, wearing cream silk dress with smocking and hand-painted buttons, undergarments, socks, shoes, signed "1987 Lynne & Michael Roche Colette C55", and having original paper labels signed by the artists. The doll was made in 1987, #55 from a limited edition. $900/1200

174. Holly by Lynne and Michael Roche
15". Having slender bisque head, painted brown eyes, dark brunette human hair, all porcelain fully articulated body with wooden ball-joints, wearing maroon knit tunic dress with white embroidery, carrying matching bag with two little yarn dolls, knit stockings, maroon leather shoes, signed "c. 1997 Lynne & Michael Roche, Holly, 1997 Collector's Club 35/1000" and having original paper label signed by the artist. $800/1100

175. Hannah by Lynne and Michael Roche
18". Having bisque head, blue glass eyes, long blonde human hair wig, all-wooden ball-jointed body with bisque swivel hands, wearing pink knit sweater with green buttons, patterned pink cotton skirt over long petticoat, panties, socks, shoes, marked "medium Hannah 1993 255" on head, and having original paper label signed by the artist. $900/1200

The Michigan artist created most of her dolls in the early 1980's. Each was hand-sculpted by the artist, without the use of molds, and thus each model can be said to be truly unique. The dolls, often representing historical or legendary figures, were based upon historical documents concerning their appearance, costumes and presence, and each is notable for its superb porcelain details of jewelry or elaborate coiffure. The artist is no longer making dolls.

176. Little Girl by Kathy Redmond
12". Having bisque shoulder head with very expressive facial features, painted eyes with decorative glaze, light brown human hair, softly stuffed muslin body, porcelain lower arms and long slender legs, painted bobby socks and black Mary Jane's, wearing pink and white striped dress, cutwork apron, petticoat, pantalets, with original Redmond logo stamped on doll, and with two original paper labels by the artist describing her porcelain technique. $400/500

177. Egyptian Family by Kathy Redmond
6" – 18". Three dolls representing man, woman and child, are of hand-pressed porcelain with individual details of sculpted accessories. The baby is all porcelain with jointed arms and wears a gold cap with decorative green serpent and lavish gold collar and beads. The man is porcelain to waist, with porcelain arms and lower legs, muslin midriff and upper legs; his headdress is decorated with coiled serpent, there is a falcon on his chest, and he wears extensive gilded jewelry. The woman, with shoulderhead turned sharply to the right wears a gold beaded coronet decorated with sea horse and winged bird; she wears extensive colored porcelain jewelry. The woman is hand-signed "Egyptian" and each doll has Redmond signature logo. $600/900

178. Napoleon and Josephine by Kathy Redmond

15" – 17". Two dolls of hand-pressed porcelain represent Josephine and Napoleon of France. She has sculpted brown hair with detailed ringlet curls and painted tendrils of curls around the forehead, gold crown and elaborate gold and jade jewelry, modeled throat hollow and bosom, porcelain lower arms and legs, gold sandaled feet with petal decorations, and wears an elegant gown. He has very detailed sculpting of darkened complexion, modeled hat with glazed black and gold colors, impasto edging to simulate ribbons, sculpted upper jacket, porcelain hands and lower legs, painted white stockings and black shoes, and wears authentically tailored uniform. They are hand-signed "Napoleon" or "Josephine" and each doll has Redmond signature logo. $600/900

179. Maximilian and Carlotta by Kathy Redmond

15" – 16". Two dolls of hand-pressed porcelain represent the last emperor and empress of Mexico. She has long flowing brown ringlet curls low onto her shoulders and topped by a gold crown studded with green jade stone, gold link necklaces and gold edged bodice, porcelain lower arms and legs, black painted shoes, and wears rich gilt brocade and lace gown. He has majestically graying hair, parted at the center, with long sideburns, moustache and flowing beard, sculpted white shirt with black bow and gold royal symbol, and wears red and cream regimental uniform with gold braid, carries sceptre. They are hand-signed "Maximilian" or "Carlotta" and each doll has Redmond signature logo. $600/900

180. Guinevere by Kathy Redmond

15". Of hand-pressed porcelain with exceptional detail of sculpting of coiffe, hair and hair ornaments, long coiled loops of hair onto the shoulders intertwined with gold beads, gold-tipped white snood, and an elaborate white scarf topped with rolled colorful ribbons as a crown; with sculpted gold "lace" bodice trimmed with jewels, porcelain lower arms and legs, wearing blue velvet gown with metallic gold braid trim. The doll is hand-signed "Guinevere" and has Redmond signature logo. $400/500

181. Richard The Lion-Hearted by Kathy Redmond

14". Of hand-pressed porcelain portraying a handsome blonde-haired man with flowing hair, side-burns and short beard, gold crown with jewels, glazed porcelain shoulder plate with elaborately sculpted cross and jewels, porcelain lower arms and legs with unusual pattern, wearing turquoise velvet tunic with gilded metallic trim. The doll is hand-signed "Richard the Lion-Hearted" and has Redmond signature logo. $400/500

182. Barry Lyndon by Kathy Redmond

15". Of hand-pressed porcelain, the figure depicts the Irish rake depicted in the 19th century Thackeray novel, having darkened complexion, wind-blown long curly hair, glazed porcelain brown tricorn hat and sculpted shirt with ruffled, bisque hands and lower legs with painted white stockings and black buckle shoes, wearing brown velvet suit with printed velvet vest. The doll is hand-signed "Barry Lyndon" and has Redmond signature logo. $400/500

183. Abigail Adams by Kathy Redmond

15". Of hand-pressed glazed porcelain, the lady has extravagant sculpting of grayish hair with long ringlet curls onto nape of neck, sculpted wide-brimmed purple hat with sienna and teal ribbons and lavish feathers, sculpted gold bear earrings, sculpted bodice with bow-trimmed blouse, glazed porcelain hands and lower legs with painted shoes, patterned flowered dress with purple vest sash. The doll is hand-signed "Abigail Adams daughter" and has Redmond signature logo. $400/500

184. Estella by Kathy Redmond

15". Of hand-pressed glazed porcelain, the slender-faced lady with smiling expression has blonde sculpted hair in arranged ringlet curls under sculpted blue poke bonnet with white ruffled edging and white flower trim, beautiful sculpted bare shoulders, porcelain hands and lower legs, blue shoes, ivory brocade gown. The doll is hand-signed "Estella" and has Redmond signature logo. $400/500

185. Mr. Carney by Kathy Redmond
18". Of hand pressed porcelain with deeply defined handsome features of older gentleman, grey tousled hair, beard and moustache under glazed porcelain black top hat, sculpted shirt collar and bow tie, bisque hands and lower legs with painted white stockings and black shoes with sculpted grey spats, gold bead buttons, wearing black velvet coat, patterned vest, trousers. The doll is hand-signed "Mr. Carney" and has Redmond signature logo. $400/500

186. Adelaid and Adelaide 2 by Kathy Redmond
Each 17". Each is of hand-pressed porcelain with varying facial expressions, one with long blonde hair interwoven with beads and surmounted by tall elaborate crown, gold bead earrings and necklace, sculpted bodice ornamentation, and wearing brown velvet gown; the other with sculpted auburn hair with beads, tall crown decorated with gilded precious "jewels", ribbons, and tassels, necklaces, lace-sculpted bodice with teal ruffle, bisque hands, bisque lower legs with shoes, wearing green velvet gown with gilt metallic trim. The dolls are hand-signed "Adelaid" and "Adelaid 2" and have Redmond signature logo. $400/500

187. Isabella of Portugal by Kathy Redmond
16". Of hand-pressed porcelain with reddish hair in loop curls under elaborate silver coiffe decorated with silver beads, gold snood at back of head, very ornate high ruffled collar with faux-diamond insets, gold edged bodice with medallion, bisque hands and lower legs, gold decorated orange shoes, grey gown with gilt metallic and pearls. The doll is hand-signed "Isabella of Portugal" and has Redmond signature logo. $400/500

188. Elizabeth I by Kathy Redmond

16". Of hand-pressed porcelain with elaborately sculpted reddish hair gathered behind sculpted ears, decorated with strands of beads and clasped by a gold snood, jewel on forehead and matching earrings, very elaborate white ruffled neck collar, stand-up decorated collar and necklace, bisque hands with many rings, bisque lower legs with fancy shoes, gold brocade gown, wooden sceptre. The doll is hand-signed "Elizabeth I" and has Redmond signature logo. $500/700

189. Berengavia by Kathy Redmond

15". Of hand-pressed porcelain, the woman with darkened complexion has sculpted flowing dark curly hair under glazed purple draped scarf with copper-tinted lining, and surmounted by a faux-jeweled gold crown, with very ornate necklace, bisque hands with jeweled rings, bisque lower legs. The doll is hand-signed "Berengavia" and has Redmond signature logo. $400/500

190. Elain by Kathy Redmond

15". Of hand-pressed glazed porcelain, woman with wide beaming smile wears a very elaborate Medieval style coiffe with gilt and blue trim from which cascades a real human hair braid, sculpted lace drape on her upper bodice with jewel buttons, porcelain hands and lower legs, wearing bronze silk gown with brocade trim. The doll is hand-signed "Elain" and has Redmond signature logo. $400/500

191. Phyllis Wheatley of Bicentennial Series by Kathy Redmond

14". Of hand-pressed brown-complexioned bisque, the woman has sharply chiseled features of character face, glazed highlights of eyes, black sculpted hair captured under a decorated white cap, bisque forearms and lower legs, wearing red cotton gown with white apron. The doll is hand-signed "Phyllis Wheatley" and "Bicentennial Series '76" and has Redmond signature logo. $400/500

192. Young Boy by Heloise
20". Wax shoulder head of young boy with slender face and elongated throat, strongly shaped facial features, green inset eyes with glazed overlay, closed mouth, brunette mohair wig, muslin torso and upper limbs, wax lower limbs, wearing artist made white shirt with tie, blue knee-length pants, socks, saddle shoes, signed Heloise on shoulder plate and "Heloise 89" on torso. The doll was made in 1989 by the French artist, Heloise, whose dolls are included in Musee des Arts Decoratifs in Paris, and who has been featured in more then ten doll artist books. $900/1300

193. Doris by Hildegard Gunzel
28". Wax-coated porcelain doll with swivel head, blue glass eyes, real inset lashes, slightly parted lips with molded teeth, delicate blushing, auburn wig, muslin torso, wax over porcelain limbs with legs posed in seated position, arms bent at elbows, wearing peach and silk dress designed by the artist, signed "Doris, H. Gunzel, 1989" on head, and "Hildegard Gunzel 1991" on torso; included is document signed by the German artist indicating that the doll is one-of-a-kind. $1600/1900

194. Wax Puppenkind by Sonja Hartmann
20". Wax swivel head with very characterized
features, large blue eyes, pointy nose, closed
mouth, blonde mohair wig in delicate braids and
tendril curls, wax shoulder plate, arms with jointed
shoulders, wax lower legs, muslin torso, wearing
lavender silk-like mariner costume, undergarments,
socks, shoes, signed "Sonja Hartmann 5/5", along
with original labeled box. $500/900

195. Kleinkind Klein Wax Doll by Brigitte Deval
19". Wax over porcelain shoulder head doll portraying a young child, has blue inset
eyes, dreamy expression, slightly parted lips, brunette mohair wig, muslin body with
gusset-jointing to allow sitting or standing, wax over porcelain lower arms and legs,
wearing rose silk dress with tiny rose appliqué petals, undergarments, stockings,
shoes, signed "1989 Brigitte Starezewski Deval, Kleinkind klein 27/100, To Monica"
on body, and signed by the artist on the head. The doll was made by the Italian
artist, Brigitte Deval in 1989 from a series of 100 dolls. $1200/1500

The designs of the American doll artist, Wendy Lawton, are made in her own studio workshops in California. Debuting in 1982, the dolls often represent persons from well-loved children's stories, fairy tales, or historical figures of special interest to children. The dolls are created in very limited numbers, with unique sculpts for each doll, and with meritorious selection of accessories that help tell the doll's story.

196. Secret Garden by Wendy Lawton

9" doll. Having bisque socket head, very dark blue inset eyes, closed mouth, blonde human hair wig, all-wooden fully-articulated body with bisque swivel-wrist hands, wearing blue silk dress with appliqué flowers, pantalets, black leggings, kidskin ankle boots, and arranged in book-shaped fabric-lined box along with blue coat, flowered apron, straw hat and flower-filled basket, nest of robin's eggs, pots, watering can. The doll is incised "Lawton 2000" and numbered 78/175. A certificate of authenticity is included in the box, and the doll has hang tag indicating "Lawton Library Collection" and original storage box. A copy of the book, The Secret Garden, is included. The doll was made in 2000 in an edition of 175. $500/800

197. Henrietta and Hilda by Wendy Lawton

17" and 8". Larger doll has bisque socket head, large brown inset eyes, upturned nose, closed mouth, red braids and curly bangs, all-wooden fully articulated body, bisque swivel-wrists hands, wearing cotton flowered dress over white blouse, petticoat, pantalets, black strap shoes, large hair bow to matching dress, and holding all-bisque baby doll with painted facial features, blonde curly hair, elaborate baby gown and jacket, modeling as antique Hilda baby. The doll is ink-signed "AP2/350" and incised "Lawton c.1996". and has original wrist booklet. The doll is artist proof from the 1996 edition of 350. $500/800

198. Amber Autumn by Wendy Lawton

13". All-bisque doll portraying a young child has swivel head, brown inset eyes, closed mouth, painted freckles, jointed bisque arms and legs, reddish-gold curly hair with elaborate side braids, wearing flowered cotton dress and russet velvet coat with matching lining, russet beret, undergarments, red knit stockings, brown leather shoes, and carrying brown leather school satchel. The doll is hand lettered "220/500" and signed by the artist, and is sold along with her "Amber Autumn" box. $400/600

199. Alice Through the Looking Glass, Collector's Guild Doll

16". Bisque socket head with heart-shaped facial modeling, large blue upper glancing inset eyes, pointy nose, closed mouth, long blonde curly hair, all-wooden fully-articulated body, bisque swivel-wrist hands, wearing blue cotton dress with white ruffled two-pocket pinafore, petticoat, pantalets, striped stockings, black shoes, and carrying a double-headed bisque baby (a piglet head on one side, a baby head on the other side); a glass bottle with label "Drink Me" is in her pocket, signed "160/180" and incised "Lawton c. 1995" on head, with hang tag "Lawton Collectors Guild Convention, Through the Looking Glass, c.1995". The doll has her original labeled box, certificate of authenticity and owns an original wooden hand mirror and miniature porcelain tea set each labeled with convention 1995 indicia. $600/900

200. The Fantastic Danielle by Wendy Lawton

13". Young girl with bisque socket head, brown inset eyes, closed mouth, softly rounded nose and cheeks, long brunette human hair wig, all-wooden fully articulated body, bisque swivel-wrist hands, wearing olive green silk dress under brown silk capelet coat, straw bonnet, petticoat, pantalets, leggings, black ankle boots. The doll is inked "34/750" and incised "Lawton" on head, and has original hang tag and original labeled box with certificate of authenticity. Included with the doll is wooden camera on tripod base, painter's box with paints, brush and palette, sketch book, an extra ensemble, and book, The Fantastic Danielle. The doll was a 1998 Doty Award nominee. $600/900

201. Only Olivia by Wendy Lawton

9". Brown-complexioned bisque socket head, brown glass eyes, closed mouth with broadly beaming smile, black fleecy hair with long braids, all-wooden fully articulated body, bisque swivel-wrist hands, wearing rose silk dress with lace ruffles and appliqués, pantalets, high stockings, pink leather shoes, pink hair bow, ink signed "155/250" and incised "Lawton c.2000" on head, with hang tag and certificate of authenticity labeled "Merely Me Collection, Only Olivia c. 2000, 155/250", tag in dress, labeled box. $400/500

202. Mirette on the High Wire by Wendy Lawton

14". Young girl having bisque socket head, brown inset eyes, closed mouth, auburn long curly wig, all-wooden fully articulated body, bisque swivel-wrist hands, wearing blue silk sailor dress, petticoat, pantalets, leggings, white boots, signed "107/750" in ink on head, incised "Lawton c.1998" on head, with hang tag "Children's Literature, Mirette on the High Wire", and dress tag "the Lawton Doll Company. The doll has certificate of authenticity, original labeled box, and two books with stories about Mirette. $600/900

203. Clara by John Friedericy

17". Wax over porcelain shoulder head, green glass eyes, angular-shaped face with upturned nose, well-shaped throat and shoulders, beautifully painted features, slender muslin body, wax over porcelain lower arms and legs, brunette human hair, wearing white handkerchief dress with delicate embroidery, undergarments, silk sash and shoes, green silk hair ribbon, signed "F90 #13" on shoulders, with original paper label ink-signed "Clara from the Nutcracker Suite #13/25", and with original dress label. Wooden

nutcracker man is included. The works of this late California artist were individually poured, then wax-dipped and hand-finished; the costumes were of imported fine fabrics. Documentation and articles from doll journals are included. The doll was made in 1990 from an edition of 25. $800/1200

204. Florence by Lynne and Michael Roche

18". Portrait doll of young girl with chubby bisque socket head, very plump cheeks, blue glass inset eyes, closed mouth, blonde curly human hair, all-wooden fully-articulated toddler body with plump shape, bisque swivel-wrist hands, wearing green knit vest over blue cotton blouse, pleated plaid wool skirt, hooded woolen duffle coat with wooden toggle buttons and colorful plaid lining, knit colorful scarf and mittens, knit stockings, suede booties with fur edges, signed "1984 Lynne and Michael Roche, Florence 280". An early model with distinctive facial shape by the English artists. $900/1200

205. "February Calendar" by Avigail Brahms, One-of-Kind
24". Portrait of young adult lady with slender well-defined face, elongated throat
with defined shoulder blades, grey upper glancing eyes, rounded nose, closed mouth
with pensive expression on the artfully painted lips, auburn human hair, armature
shaped torso in seated position, sculpted hands and legs, wearing artist made pale
yellow crepe and tulle gown of antique fabric, with delicate ruffles, appliqué flowers,
large hair bow, signed Avigail Brahms, 1987. The artist's medium is fima, lending a
beautiful translucent quality to the doll's complexion. The one-of-a-kind doll, an
early model by this artist, 1987, was features in a calendar as February (documents
included). $2000/2500

206. Hannah by Lynne and Michael Roche
18". Bisque socket head with plump facial
modeling, blue glass eyes, delicately painted
features, closed mouth, blonde human hair long
wig, all-wooden body with ball-jointing, bisque
hands, wearing patterned cotton print dress, pink
knit sweater with doll brooch, petticoat with
checkered border, knit stockings, leather shoes,
signed "1984 Lynne & Michael Roche Medium
Hannah 35", and with original paper label. The doll
was made by the English doll artists in 1984.
$1100/1400

207. Gigi by Brigitte Deval

26". Wax over porcelain swivel head on waxed shoulder plate, blue glass inset eyes, plump cheeks modeling with delicately tinted blush, lightly painted brow, lashes and lips of clothed mouth, brunette mohair wig with soft curls, firmly stuffed muslin body, wax arms to above the bent elbows, wax lower legs with bare feet, wearing artist-made dress of sheer organdy over blue and white striped, multi-tiered cutwork yoke, petticoat, pantalets, signed "Brigitte Starczewski-Deval, Gigi, 20/28, 1987" on head and torso. The German-born Italian artist is celebrated for doll portraiture; she has noted "each one is very real – an involved and complicated personality. Yes I am a portrait painter and a sculptor, but dollmaking is my chosen medium." Gigi was #20 from a numbered edition of 28, created in 1987. $2000/2500

208. Ina by Brigitte Deval

22". Wax over porcelain swivel head on waxed shoulder plate, blue glass eyes with yellow flecks glancing slightly to the right in a wide-eyed expression, delicately oil-painted features, slightly parted lips as though in wonderment, light brown mohair wig with tendril curls, firmly-stuffed muslin body, waxed lower arms and legs, bare feet, expressively posed fingers, wearing artist-made blue taffeta dress with Bertha collar, petticoat and pantalets, signed "1987 Brigitte Starczewski Deval, Ina, 75/100". The doll was 75 from a number edition of 100, made by Deval in 1987. $1000/1500

209. Greta as Camille by Paul Crees

28". Poured wax portrait doll depicting Greta Garbo, her head haughtily tilted upward, slender face with strong chin and cheek bones, elongated neck, female-shaped wax torso, jointed long slender legs, arms fabric-jointed at shoulders; oil-painted eyes, inserted mohair lashes and painted eye decoration, richly shaded lips, light brown human hair, wearing original red taffeta gown with black lace overlay decorated with hand-painted designs and silver stars, lace embroidered scarf, rhinestone necklace, earrings, and ring, undergarments, black shoes. With original certificate "Greta Garbo, Camille, Third Edition #2/40, June 1988, Paul Crees", along with various brochures by the artist, several magazine articles described the English artist's work. Drawing upon his background in London theatrical design, and inspired by the 19th century English wax artists Pierroti and Montanari, Paul Crees has created a very limited number of his masterpiece works. $1200/1800

210. Beauty and the Beast by Pat Thompson

24" Beast, 31" Beauty. Each porcelain doll portrays the theatrical figure, the beast with brown complexion and deeply wizened features, glazed brown eyes to simulate glass, sculpted open mouth with two fangs, very thick human hair, muslin body, bisque hands with elongated fingers and feet with painted two-tone shoes, wearing tweed pants, richly feathered collar; the beauty with blue glass inset eyes, real lashes, delicately painted features, closed mouth, brunette human hair, shapely muslin body, bisque lower arms and legs with sculpted fancy high heeled shoes, very elaborate ivory crepe gown with lace and flower appliqués, taffeta petticoat and pantalets. The beast is signed "Vlasta 11", and there is a paper label on the beauty "Vlasta Dolls, Original Pat Thompson sculpture #6 series of 100, Beauty and the Beast 75, 2/20". The pair were #2 from an edition of 20 sets created in the mid-1980's in the studio of the Illinois artist Pat Thompson. $1200/1700

211. Klara by Hildegard Gunzel

32". Wax-over-porcelain swivel head, brown glass inset eyes in half-moon shape, delicately painted brows, lashes, and lips, impressed philtrum and dimples, blonde human hair with side braids, muslin body, wax over-porcelain lower arms and legs, expressively posed fingers and toes, wearing artist made airy blue silk dress with silver metallic sleeves, with antique fabric banner decorated with silver metallic encrustations, signed Hildegard Gunzel, Klara 1987. $1200/1700

212. Resli by Hildegard Gunzel

27". Wax over porcelain swivel head depicting an older child with elongated throat and face, blue glass inset eyes, painted features with slightly upturned nose and delicate freckles, closed mouth, brunette mohair curly wig, muslin body, waxed arms and legs, bent knees designed for sitting, posed curled toes of bare feet, wearing artist made hand-painted dress with smocking and lace bretelles, cotton one-piece undergarment, signed Resli 100/87. The German doll artist began her career in fashion design, and began creating porcelain dolls in the early 1980's. Soon thereafter she introduced the medium, wax-over-porcelain, in which she was able to best express the ephemeral beauty of youth. $1000/1400

213. Katchha by Pat Thompson

22". Bisque swivel head on bisque shoulder plate portraying a young girl with very full cheeks, blue glass eyes, real lashes, delicate blushing on nose tip, chin and cheeks, blonde human hair, muslin torso, bisque lower arms and legs, expressively posed fingers, wearing ivory silk dress under mauve silk twill coat with lace-trimmed capelet collar, matching bonnet and muff, undergarments, stockings, shoes, original paper booklet "Vlasta, Katcha #121/200" describes the doll as a portrait of Katchka, the Czar's favorite daughter, created in 1987. $1000/1300

214. Colene by Pat Thompson

22". Bisque swivel head on bisque shoulder plate portraying a young girl with high cheeks bones, point nose, blue glass eyes, real lashes, gleaming glaze on blushed cheeks, nose and chin, light brown human hair, muslin torso, bisque lower arms and legs, expressively posed fingers, wearing organza dress decorated with pulled silk ribbon and flowers, ruffled lace, embroidered linen collar and star-shaped bonnet,.matching shoes, undergarments, holding a little bisque doll, original paper booklet "Vlasta, Colene #11/50" and hand-lettered "Original Pat Thompson sculpture #3 series of 250". The doll, costumed as Colene, was made only in an edition of 50, 1987. $1000/1300

215. Daddy's Darling by Pat Thompson

22". Bisque swivel head on bisque shoulder plate portraying a young girl with very full cheeks, blue glass eyes, real lashes, delicate blushing on nose tip, chin and cheeks, upturned nose tip, blonde human hair, muslin torso, bisque lower arms and legs, expressively posed fingers, wearing rose silk dress decorated with English netting and French ribbons and lace, wide ruffled bretelles, matching bonnet that captures a cluster of ringlet curls at the back of the head, undergarments, stockings, shoes, original paper booklet "Vlasta, Daddy's Darling, 8/50" and hand-lettered "Original pat Thompson Sculpture #9 series of 250. The doll, costumed as Daddy's Darling, was made only in an edition of 50, 1987. $1000/1300.

216. Mattie by Pat Thompson

22". Bisque swivel head on bisque shoulder plate portraying a young girl with high cheeks bones, pointed nose, blue glass eyes, real lashes, gleaming glaze on blushed cheeks, nose and chin, light brown human hair, muslin torso, bisque lower arms and legs, expressively posed fingers, wearing yellow organza dress decorated with tiers of ruffles and lace, wide puffed sleeves, ruffled silk ribbon edging, matching wide bonnet, reticule, and shoes, undergarments, original paper booklet "Vlasta, Mattie 4/12" and indicating that only 12 of the dolls had been created because their costumes had been made from a very limited stock of lace found at an old wedding dress studio.The doll, costumed as Mattie, was made only in an edition of 12, 1987. $1000/1300

217. The Kite Dream by Sue McFadden

15". Firmly pressed felt head with painted facial features, small side-glancing eyes, auburn mohair wig, softly stuffed torso of older child, felt elongated limbs, wearing cotton print playsuit and matching white blouse, felt slippers and holding a quilted kite with cloth doll head, marked "KD 25/25 SM 92" on doll and "Personality Dolls" printed on tag with hand-lettered "The Kite Dream 25/25 Susan H. McFadden c.1992" on inside. $400/500

218. Olivia by Yolanda Bello

13" seated. Bisque swivel head on bisque shoulder plate, small glass eyes, highly characterized sculpting of face, rounded nose, impressed dimples, smiling expression on closed mouth, reddish blonde lambswool wig with braids, muslin torso, bisque lower arms and legs, wearing cotton checkered blouse, velvet checkered skirt, angora shawl, undergarments, shoes, socks, and posed, seated, on wooden chair. Included is original document indicating that "Olivia" is an original by Yolanda Bello, #21/250. $500/700

219. Boy in Green Sweater by Wiltrud Stein

11". Shoulder head with painted facial features depicts a young fretful boy, decorative glaze on eyes, shaded highlights between the lips, blonde mohair bobbed wig, firmly stuffed kidskin body, ceramic lower arms and legs, wearing hand-knit green sweater with wooden buttons, tan trousers, leather sandals, incised "Wiltrud: on neck and with ceramic tag "Wiltrud Puppe". The doll is one of the early works by German artists, Wiltrud Stein, who began her doll career in 1985. $500/700

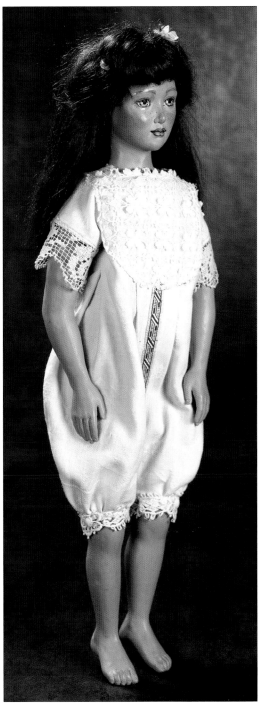

220. Karl by Phyllis Wright
15". Bisque head on bisque shoulder plate, painted brown eyes with decorative glaze to suggest glass, beautifully painted brows, blush and lips, blonde human hair, muslin torso, bisque arms and legs, wearing artist-made white pique sailor suit, woven cap with fancy streamers, stockings, black leather shoes, signed by artist and 1979 date on head, with original paper booklet "Phyllis Wright, House of Wright" and hand-lettered "Karl #1250 KB 4". $400/500

221. Jacks by Julie Good-Kruger
11". Bisque socket head on twill-over-armature shoulder plate and muslin torso, bisque arms to above the elbows, shapely bisque legs to above the knees,.painted facial features, glazed highlights on side-glancing eyes, shy expression, closed mouth, brunette wig,, wearing red cotton smock, bloomers, black leggings, brown shoes, marked "Julie Good-Kruger c. 1984 2/3 Jacks". The doll was made in a very limited edition of 3 in 1984. $400/500

222. Struwelmarie by Beate Schult
18". Fired-composition shoulder head portraying young lady, with artistically painted facial features, outlined and shaded eyes, outlined lips, fringed brow, light freckles on blushed cheeks, auburn mohair wig, firmly stuffed fabric body, fired-composition shapely arms and legs, bare feet, wearing linen one piece garment, with original paper label hand-lettered "doll No.2". The Munich doll artist is noted for art dolls made of all-leather (see #153) or a special fired-composition of her own formulation. Each doll is individually made. The artist has been creating dolls since 1975, and her works are in various museums including Musee des Arts Decoratif in Paris. $700/900

223. Bunny by Hildegard Gunzel

26". Wax over porcelain swivel head on waxed shoulder plate, amber brown glass inset eyes, real lashes, mouth modeled as though open with expressive lips, two teeth, dimpled chin, blonde human hair, muslin body, waxed baby limbs, bare feet, wearing delicate silk and tulle baby gown with orange blossom decorations, signed "Bunny, Sample (?), H. Gunzel 95" on head, and with original paper label. $900/1200

224. Resli by Hildegard Gunzel

24". Wax over porcelain swivel head on waxed shoulder plate, amber brown glass inset eyes, closed mouth, delicately painted features, brunette human hair, muslin torso, waxed limbs posed for seating, original delicate costume, signed "Resli 88 H. Gunzel" on head, "1989 Hildegard Gunzel" on torso, and with original certificate dated March 26, 1989. $800/1000

225. Little Dancer by Hildegard Gunzel

24". Wax over porcelain swivel head on wax shoulder plate with modeled bosom and elongated throat, brown glass eyes, closed mouth, blonde wig, muslin body, wax arms and legs posed as though dancing, wearing delicate sheer gown with lace trim, signed "H. Gunzel 1993" on head and "Little Dancer H. Gunzel 13" on body. $600/900

226. Girl in Pink Bonnet by Edna Daly
13". Portrait in fima of child with slender angular face tilted slightly sideways, elongated throat, auburn mohair wig with looped braids, brown glass side-glancing eyes, eye shadow, delicate freckles, closed mouth, muslin torso, wax limbs, expressive fingers, molded white socks, and pink one-strap shoes, artist-made tulle dress with double tiered ruffles, felt hat with flower trim, silk petticoat and pantalets, signed "Edna Daly 1983". Creating dolls for more than two decades, the artist has worked in fima, porcelain and wax over porcelain. Her smaller dolls, as this, are among her rarest. $800/1000

227. Allena by Ruth Treffeisen
26". Bisque swivel head on bisque shoulder plate, brown glass inset eyes, beautifully painted complexion and facial features, closed mouth with decorative glaze on lips, brunette human hair with curls and braids, muslin body, bisque lower limbs, wearing rose silk dress with embroidered white collar, petticoat, pantalets, knit stockings, leather shoes with hand-stitched trim, incised "Allena 34/100" on head, "34" on shoulder plate, "RuthT" on torso, "RuthT" on costume, with original booklet signed by the artist with production date of 1989, from a numbered series of 100 by the German artist, Ruth Treffeisen. $600/900

228. Jordan By Joanne Gelin

15". Brown-complexioned porcelain head with very expressive features, plump cheeks, painted facial features, brown eyes with glazed highlights, real side lashes, closed mouth, black mohair wig with tight curls secured by colorful ribbons, bead-filled brown muslin body, brown bisque hands with expressively posed fingers, cernit lower legs with sculpted shoes and socks, wearing artist made costume with hand-knit pink sweater decorated with colorful suede symbols, signed "Jordan 7/15 c.Joanne Gelin 1994". The doll was from a numbered edition of 15, made in 1994 by the West Virginia artist whose dolls were featured on the cover of Contemporary Doll World in 1996. $300/400

229. Asian Child by Joyce Stafford

12". Bisque swivel head with painted facial features, brown upper glancing eyes with decorative glaze, closed mouth, pouty expression, black human hair bobbed wig, double chin, muslin torso and upper limbs, bisque lower limbs, bare feet, wearing orange cotton dress, undergarments, white pinafore, orange sandals, body label "Joyce Stafford NIADA". $300/400

230. Baby by Astry Campbell

9". Solid domed bisque socket head, painted brown baby hair, painted facial features, grey upglancing eyes with decorative glaze, closed mouth, all bisque baby body, wearing white baby gown and bonnet, signed "c.Astry Campbell 1972". The all-bisque baby was made by the early NIADA artist in 1972. $200/300

230A. Boy with Hobby Horse and Piglet by Classic in Wood

12". Carved wooden socket head with carved bobbed hair, carved and painted facial features with pensive expression, all wooden fully jointed body with attached ball-joints at shoulders, elbows, hips and knees, wearing brown and white checkered shirt, brown short trousers under long linen-like tunic shirt with smocking and featherstitching, leggings, brown leather ankle boots, and holding a toy hobby horse and toy white piglet in a brown sack. The doll has original wooden button . The artist appears to have worked during the 1980's creating all-wooden dolls in editions of 100. $500/700

231. Jerry by Bob Beckett

12". Carved wooden head portraying an impish young boy, upturned nose, carved laughter lines, painted brown side-glancing eyes, closed mouth with smiling expression, light brown human hair wig, muslin stitch-jointed body, carved wooden hands, original brown and white checkered shirt, brown overalls, brown suede shoes, signed "Beckett Originals" on pants, and "12/22/80 Jerry by Bob Beckett Orig". Wooden dolls, each hand-carved by the artist couple, June and Bob Beckett of Tennessee, were made during the 1970's and 1980's; the founding members of ODACA closed their workshop in 1989. $400/500

232. Grey-Haired Woman by Patti Hale

16". Carved wooden head with well-defined carved features including eye brows, dimples, ears, eye sockets, and charming crooked nose, natural finish enhanced by soft cheek blush, painted upper glancing eyes, grey mohair wig with bun, soft muslin body, wooden hands with spread fingers, wooden lower legs with sculpted black heeled shoes, white cotton blouse with brooch, black skirt, pantalets, signed "Patti Hale NIADA '84". The sculpture was made by California artist, early NIADA member, in 1984 who wrote "I make dolls to recreate life around me in miniature, frozen in time." $400/500

233. Lucie by Nancy Bruns

22". Carved wooden head with expressive laughing features, painted blue eyes, mouth carved as though open with row of painted teeth, flower-printed fabric body, carved wooden hands and bare feet, blonde wig, cotton jumper, homespun blouse, pantalets, signed ""c.1986 Nancy P. Bruns 85 Lucie Maple" on head, Brunswood Doll and Lucie cloth tags on dress, original paper booklet. The Ohio artist, Nancy Bruns hand-carved and painted each of her dolls of fine native woods, Lucie being made of maple wood. $500/700

234. Malcolm by Nancy Bruns

22". Carved wooden head with uniquely carved features, darkened complexion, brown painted eyes, beaming smile with painted teeth and carved dimples, black tightly curled hair, cloth body of tiny blue and white checkered muslin, carved wooden hands and bare feet, wearing cotton checkered shirt with wooden buttons, black short pants with suspenders, woolen cap, spectacles, black bow tie, signed "c. 1986 Nancy P. Bruns, 38 Malcolm Cherry", original cloth tags "Brunswood Doll" and "Malcolm" on costumes, and original paper booklet indicating that Malcolm was made of cherrywood. The doll was given an Award of Excellence in 1990. $500/700

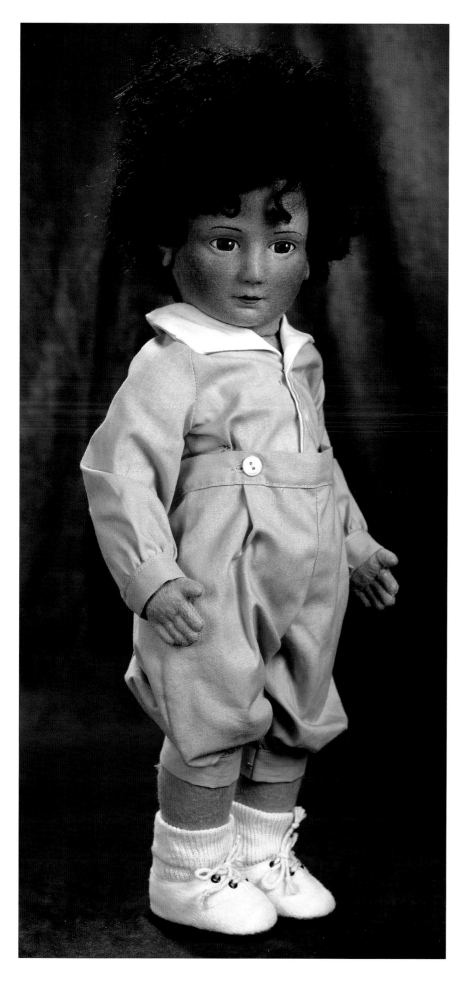

235. William by R. John Wright, Number One of the Model

17". Felt swivel head with pressed and painted facial features, brown eyes, softly blushed features, painted lashes, eyeliner, nostrils, and mouth, brunette curly mohair wig, jointed felt arms and legs, wearing blue cotton romper suit with white collar, socks, white felt shoes, artist-signed "Wright" on foot, original paper label "R. John Wright Little Children Series I William" with ink-signed notation "W3-1/250", in original labeled box "w-3", with NIADA certificate of authenticity, and with hand-written note by R. John Wright noting "Congratulations, you are the lucky owner of the very first William ever made...". William was released in 1981, from a numbered edition of 250. $1100/1500

236. Pair, Lisa and Scott by R. John Wright, Matched Numbered Set

Each 17". The young boy and girl are costumed as though twins, each with felt swivel head with pressed and painted facial features, he with painted blue eyes and she with painted brows eyes, fine detail of pressed sculpting of eye sockets, mouth, and chin, each with strawberry blonde mohair wig, he with curly hair, she with tiny braids, each with five piece felt body, wearing matching costumes featuring white shirts, colorfully hand-knit sweaters in red and magenta, grey woolen skirt or shorts, knit socks, brown leather ankle shoes, he with leather school bag and magenta knit cap, she carrying a white mohair cat with green glass eyes. Each is signed "R. John Wright" on the foot, has original paper label "R. John Wright Little Children Series II, Lisa (or Scott) No/176/250" and has original labeled box. The matched numbered dolls were issued in 1985-86. $2000/2500

237. The Mouse Tailor by R. John Wright, Collector's Club Exclusive

4" with spool. Shaded brown mohair mouse with long tail, glass eyes, brown felt paws and felt-lined shaded ears, spectacles is seated atop a spool of thread with RJW label on the base, reading a little booklet "The Tailor and Cutter", with original paper label "Beatrix Potter, The Mouse Tailor, #87, R. John Wright", original certificate of authenticity indicating #87 from the piece produced exclusively for R.Jiohn Wright Collectors Club in 2001-2002; and with original silk-lined box and story book, The Tailor of Gloucester with Beatrix Potter illustrations. Only 585 models were produced of The Mouse Tailor. $500/700

238. Periwinkle on Pincushion by R. John Wright, Collector's Club Exclusive

6" seated. Pressed felt elf Periwinkle, the symbol of the R. John Wright firm, has green felt body cover, white collar and cuffs, grey felt wings, dark green cap, elf ears, and is seated upon a red felt tomato pincushion holding a silver needle with blue thread, with original label "Periwinkle #122" and contained in original box with certificate of authenticity. The piece was made as a Collector's Club exclusive in 1998; 807 were made. $400/500

239. Johnny Town Mouse by R. John Wright

3". Shaded brown mohair mouse with pink felt-lined ears, resin paws, bead eyes, long tail, wearing blue felt jacket and yellow vest, original paper label "Beatrix Potter Johnny Town Mouse #149", certificate of authenticity, storybook "The Tale of Johnny Town-Mouse", and contained in original box. The piece was made as a Collector's Club exclusive in 2003. $400/500

240. Pair, Jack and Jill by R. John Wright, Exclusive Editions

Each 17". Young boy and girl, each with felt swivel head with pressed and painted facial features, painted brown eyes, solemn expression with softly blushed cheeks and lips, she with dark brunette hair held by green felt hair bows, he with tousled red mohair wig, each with five piece felt body, he wearing brown homespun jacket with smocking, black felt shorts and shoes, orange and black striped stockings, she wearing yellow dress with white felt appliqués and smocking, slip, bloomers, green and black striped stockings, orange felt hat, with wooden bucket. Each doll has original paper label on costume indicating 24/100, RJW button, original wrist booklet with nursery rhyme, Jack and Jill, and they are contained in double-size box with original R. John Wright ABC paper label. The Nursery Rhyme set is #24 from the numbered series of 100 pairs released in 1992-1993 exclusively for The Toy Shoppe. $2000/2500

241. Set of Nine Dolls, Two Snow White Dolls and Seven Dwarves, by R. John Wright

16" and 9". Each has pressed felt head with painted facial features as the character appeared in the Walt Disney film, each figure with a different facial expression. The Dwarves have white mohair beards and felt costumes, and the set also includes Snow White as "Rags" with patched felt costume, bucket and scrub brush, and "Princess" in royal costume. Each piece has original RJW button, paper label indicating "Walt Disney (name of character) 71/3500 R. John Wright" except "Rags" whose tag reads "#71/1000". Each figure has original labeled box. The set was released in 1989 and produced until 1994; only 2500 sets were made, and "Rags" was made in an edition of 1000. Each of the dolls in this group is numbered #71, from the original year of production, and are a matched set. $3500/4500

INDEX OF ARTISTS

Note: Reference numbers refer to the doll number, not the page number

Adams, Christine 155
Aneelin, Maloy 154
Augustin, Almut 148, 149
Beckett, Bob 231
Bello, Yolando 218
Brahms, Avigail 205
Bruns, Nancy 233, 234
Campbell, Astry 230
Classic in Wood 230
Crees, Paul 209
Daly, Edna 226
Davies, Jane 128-133
Deval, Brigitte 195, 207, 208,
Dunham, Susan 165
Friedericy, John 203
Gelin, Joanne 228
Good-Krueger, Julie 221
Gunzel, Hildegard .193, 211, 212, 223, 224, 225
Hale, Patti 232
Hartmann, Sonja 194
Heloise 192
Iacono, Maggie 156-163
Kish, Helen 164
Lawton, Wendy 196-202
McFadden, Sue 217
Natterer, Sylvia 151
Pongratz, Elisabeth 144, 145, 146
Redmond, Kathy 176-191
Roche, Lynne & Michael 168-175, 204, 206
Sandreuter, Regina 135-142
Schmitt, Karin 150
Schult, Beate 153, 222
Stafford, Joyce 229
Stein, Wiltrud 134, 219
Thompson, Pat 210, 213-216
Tonner, Robert 152
Treffeisen, Ruth 227
Wall, Patricia 143
Walters, Nancy 166
Wright, J. John 1-128, 235-241
Wright, Phyllis 220